POEMS

POEMS

Emily Brontë

Introduction by Robert Van de Weyer

Fount
An Imprint of HarperCollinsPublishers

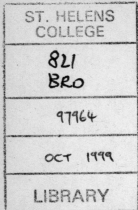
Fount Paperbacks is an Imprint of
HarperCollins*Religious*
Part of HarperCollins*Publishers*
77–85 Fulham Palace Road, London W6 8JB

This edition first published in Great Britain
in 1996 by Fount Paperbacks

1   3   5   7   9   10   8   6   4   2

Copyright © in the Introduction 1996
by Robert Van de Weyer

A catalogue record for this book is
available from the British Library

ISBN 0 00 627994 5

Printed and bound in Great Britain by
Caledonian International Book Manufacturing Ltd, Glasgow, G64

Contents

Introduction

As the daughter of an Anglican parson, and having been brought up by an aunt who was staunchly Methodist, religion dominated Emily Brontë's formative years. As a child and as an adult she wrote poetry that is shot through with spiritual yearning and with a sense of the divine, putting her amongst the greatest religious poets of the English language. Yet she deeply disliked formal religion and recoiled from those – like her aunt – whose souls were caught up in the doctrines and attitudes of religious orthodoxy; she wrote of religion as a 'brotherhood of misery with smiles as sad as sighs'. Her poetry is a celebration of the divine presence within nature, and she speaks of worshipping at Nature's 'shrine'. To her the root of all suffering is the spiritual alienation of the individual from the divine spirit of creation; and joy consists in the unity of the individual spirit with the spirit of the natural order.

In 1820, when Emily was aged two, her father became rector of Haworth, a bleak village on the Yorkshire moors. A year later her mother died, and her mother's sister moved into the rectory to supervise domestic arrangements and to educate Emily and her two sisters Charlotte and Anne. Although the aunt tried to impose strict discipline, their father encouraged his daughters to roam freely on the moors. They invented two fantasy worlds, Gondal and Angria. Their father provided books of all kinds to stimulate their minds, and even gave them newspapers. For a brief period Charlotte and Emily were sent to a boarding school in Lancashire, whose harsh discipline is vividly described in Charlotte's novel *Jane Eyre*. Later, Emily was sent to another school near Huddersfield. But on both occasions she was so miserable that her father took her home after a few months. At the age of 20 Emily spent six months as a teacher in Halifax; but here too she became so depressed and homesick that she was forced to resign her post. In 1842 she and Charlotte went to Brussels to learn French and German, with a view to opening a school of their own. Charlotte enjoyed this new environment, but Emily's shyness prevented her from making friends, and she hated urban life, longing for the freedom of the moors. Their aunt's death later that year compelled them to return home; Emily spent the rest of her short life in Haworth, keeping house for her father. She died of consumption in December 1848, and her sister Anne died a few months later.

The life of these three remarkable sisters in Haworth has been portrayed in numerous books and films over the past century and a half; the rectory is usually described as dark and gloomy, and Emily as melancholic and taciturn. In fact, according to a family friend, the interior decoration in the rectory was bright and cheerful: 'the hall and stairs were done with sandstone, always beautifully clean, as was everything about the house; the walls were . . . stained a pretty dove-grey tint . . . elegance and refinement diffused themselves over all.' The same observer described Emily as 'stout and hearty', recalling that within the family she was nicknamed 'the Major' because she organized the household with military precision. But to outsiders her shyness made her seem distant and even discourteous. According to Charlotte, Emily was shy even with the villagers, observing their behaviour closely with the artist's eye and ear, but not befriending them: 'She knew them, knew their ways, their language, their family histories; she would talk of them with detail, minute, graphic, and accurate; but with them she rarely exchanged a word.'

Behind her heartiness towards the family and shyness to strangers lay a restless and turbulent imagination. After her household duties were finished she spent many hours walking across the moors, or sitting down in some lonely spot, contemplating the rocks and grass around her and the 'glorious sphere' above. In her novel *Shirley*, Charlotte describes this aspect of her sister's life: 'In her nature prevailed at times an easy indolence. There were periods when she took delight in perfect vacancy of hand and eye – moments when her thoughts, her simple existence, the fact of the world being around – and heaven above her, seemed to yield her such fulness of happiness, that she did not need to lift a finger to increase the joy. Often, after an active morning, she would spend a sunny afternoon lying stirless on the turf . . . no spectacle did she ask but that of the deep blue sky, and such cloudlets as sailed afar and aloft across the span; no sound but that of a bee's hum, the leaf's whisper. Her sole book in such hours was the dim chronicle of memory, or the sibyl page of anticipation . . . round her lips at moments played a smile which revealed glimpses of the tale or prophecy; it was not sad, not dark.'

In those indolent hours alone the novel on which her fame rests, *Wuthering Heights*, was conceived. As David Cecil has written, conventional notions of good and evil play little or no part in the book; and formal religion is represented by the miserly and misanthropic figure of Joseph, who nightly counts out his grubby pound notes on an open Bible, and who consistently calls on his Maker to judge and punish his many enemies. The characters are caught in a cosmic struggle to find serenity out of rage, peace out of conflict, harmony out of disorder, and love out of hate. Through her portrayal of this struggle the author is reaching towards a spiritual wisdom which transcends the creeds and doctrines of orthodox Christianity. In this sense *Wuthering Heights* is a work of profound mysticism.

This mystical vision is expressed more clearly and explicitly in her poetry. She penetrated the world of the human soul and also the spirit of Nature. This exploration is gentle and tender, as if she is aware of the frailty of the soul. But the deeper she goes, the harder is the spiritual conflict she finds. At times she yearns for the darkness and coldness of death, as the only escape from inner torment; yet at these moments of despair she finds light and warmth. Occasionally her poetry rises to great heights of joy, as she 'senses the divine breath' which 'enlivens' every soul and every living creature.

It took some decades for the genius of *Wuthering Heights* to be appreciated by the general public; now it is universally acknowledged as a masterpiece. Her poetry initially suffered from being published with the rather indifferent verses of her two sisters, and then it was overshadowed by her novel. But today, as the mystical writings of all religions grow in popularity, her poetry deserves a much wider readership. The critic Philip Henderson has rightly compared her poems, in their vision and imagery, to those of St John of the Cross. When she writes:

'My outward sense is gone, my inward essence feels –
Its wings are almost free, its home, its harbour, found;
Measuring the gulf it stoops and dares the final bound!'

she is using language which the great masters of prayer throughout the ages would instantly recognize.

ROBERT VAN DE WEYER

POEMS

WOODS, YE NEED NOT FROWN ON ME

Woods, ye need not frown on me –
Spectral trees, that so dolefully
Shake your heads in the dreary sky,
Ye need not mock so bitterly!

1836

REDBREAST, EARLY IN THE MORNING

Redbreast, early in the morning
Dank and cold and cloudy grey,
Wildly tender is thy music,
Chasing angry thought away.

My heart is not enraptured now,
My eyes are full of tears,
And constant sorrow on my brow
Has done the work of years.

It was not Hope that wrecked at once
The spirit's calm in storm,
But a long life of solitude,
Hopes quenched and rising thoughts subdued,
A bleak November's calm.

What woke it then? A little child
Strayed from its father's cottage door,
And in the hour of moonlight wild
Laid lonely on the desert moor.

I heard it then, you heard it too,
And seraph-sweet it sang to you:
But like the shriek of misery
That wild, wild music wailed to me!

February 1837

THERE SHINES THE MOON

There shines the moon, at noon of night,
Vision of glory – Dream of light!
Holy as heaven – undimmed and pure,
Looking down on the lonely moor –
And lonelier still beneath her ray
That drear moor stretches far away
Till it seems strange that ought can lie
Beyond its zone of silver sky.

Bright moon – dear moon! when years have past
My weary feet return at last –
And still upon Lake Elnor's breast
Thy solemn rays serenely rest
And still the fern-leaves sighing wave
Like mourners over Elbë's grave
And Earth's the same but oh to see
How wildly Time has altered me!
Am I the being who long ago
Sat watching by that water side
The light of life expiring slow
From his fair cheek and brow of pride?

Not oft these mountains feel the shine
Of such a day – as, fading then,
Cast from its fount of gold divine
A last smile on the heathery plain,
And kissed the far-off peaks of snow
That gleaming on the horizon shone
As if in summer's warmest glow
Stern winter claimed a loftier throne.
And there he lay among the bloom
His red blood dyed a deeper hue,
Shuddering to feel the ghostly gloom

That coming Death around him threw –
Sickening to think one hour would sever
The sweet, sweet world and him for ever,
To think that twilight gathering dim
Would never pass away to him –
No – never more! That awful thought
A thousand dreary feelings brought,
And memory all her powers combined
And rushed upon his fainting mind.
Wide, swelling woodlands seemed to rise
Beneath soft, sunny, southern skies –
Old Elbë Hall, his noble home,
Towered mid its trees, whose foliage green
Rustled with the kind airs that come
From summer heavens when most serene –
And bursting through the leafy shade
A gush of golden sunshine played;
Bathing the walls in amber light
And sparkling in the water clear
That stretched below – reflected bright
The whole wide world of cloudless air.
And still before his spirit's eye
Such well-known scenes would rise and fly
Till, maddening with despair and pain
He turned his dying face to me.
And wildly cried, 'Oh once again
'Might I my native country see!
'But once again – one single day!
'And must it – can it *never* be?
'To die – and die so far away
'When life has hardly smiled for me.
'Augusta, you will soon return
'Back to that land in health and bloom
'And then the heath alone will mourn
'Above my unremembered tomb,

'For you'll forget the lonely grave
'And mouldering corpse by Elnor's wave.'
6 March 1837

ALL DAY I'VE TOILED

All day I've toiled, but not with pain,
In learning's golden mine;
And now at eventide again
The moonbeams softly shine.

There is no snow upon the ground,
No frost on wind or wave:
The south wind blew with gentlest sound
And broke their icy grave.

'Tis sweet to wander here at night
To watch the winter die,
With heart as summer sunshine light
And warm as summer sky.

O may I never lose the peace
That lulls me gently now,
Though time should change my youthful
face,
And years should shade my brow!

True to myself, and true to all,
May I be healthful still,
And turn away from passion's call,
And curb my own wild will.

1837 (?)

I AM THE ONLY BEING WHOSE DOOM

I am the only being whose doom
No tongue would ask, no eye would mourn;
I never caused a thought of gloom,
A smile of joy, since I was born.

In secret pleasure, secret tears,
This changeful life has slipped away,
As friendless after eighteen years,
As lone as on my natal day.

There have been times I cannot hide,
There have been times when this was drear,
When my sad soul forgot its pride
And longed for one to love me here.

But those were in the early glow
Of feelings since subdued by care,
And they have died so long ago
I hardly now believe they were.

First melted off the hope of youth
Then fancy's rainbow fast withdrew,
And then experience told me truth
In mortal bosoms never grew.

'Twas grief enough to think mankind
All hollow, servile, insincere –
But worse to trust to my own mind
And find the same corruption there.

17 May 1837

I SAW THEE, CHILD, ONE SUMMER'S DAY

I saw thee, child, one summer's day
Suddenly leave thy cheerful play,
And in the green grass, lowly lying,
I listened to thy mournful sighing.

I knew the wish that waked that wail:
I knew the source whence sprung those tears;
You longed for fate to raise the veil
That darkened over coming years.

The anxious prayer was heard, and power
Was given me, in that silent hour,
To open to an infant eye
The portals of futurity.

But, child of dust, the fragrant flowers,
The bright blue sky and velvet sod
Were strange conductors to the bowers
Thy daring footsteps must have trod.

I watched my time, and summer passed,
And Autumn waning fleeted by,
And doleful Winter nights at last
In cloudy mourning clothed the sky.

And now I've come: this evening fell
Not stormily, but stilly drear;
A sound sweeps o'er thee like a knell
To banish joy and welcome care;

A fluttering blast that shakes the leaves
And whistles round the gloomy wall,
And lingering long lamenting grieves,
For it is the spectre's call.

He hears me: what a sudden start
Sent the blood icy to that heart;
He wakens, and how ghastly white
That face looks in the dim lamplight.

Those tiny hands in vain essay
To thrust the shadowy fiend away:
There is a horror on his brow,
An anguish in his bosom now:

A fearful anguish in his eyes
Fixed strainedly on the vacant air;
Heavily bursts in long-drawn sighs
His panting breath, enchained by fear.

Poor child, if spirits such as I
Could weep o'er human misery,
A tear might flow, aye, many a tear,
To see the road that lies before,
To see the sunshine disappear,
And hear the stormy waters roar,
Breaking upon a desolate shore,
Cut off from hope in early day,
From power and glory cut away.

But it is doomed, and morning's light
Must image forth the scowl of night,
And childhood's flower must waste its bloom
Beneath the shadow of the tomb.

July 1837

O GOD OF HEAVEN! THE DREAM OF HORROR

O God of Heaven! the dream of horror,
The frightful dream is over now;
The sickened heart, the blasting sorrow,
The ghastly night, the ghastlier morrow,
The aching sense of utter woe;

The burning tears that would keep welling,
The groans that mocked at every tear
That burst from out their dreary dwelling,
As if each gasp were life expelling,
But life was nourished by despair;

The tossing and the anguished pining;
The grinding teeth and staring eye;
The agony of still repining,
When not a spark of hope was shining
From gloomy fate's relentless sky;

The impatient rage, the useless shrinking
From thoughts that yet could not be borne;
The soul that was for ever thinking,
Till nature, maddened, tortured, sinking,
At last refused to mourn –

It's over now – and I am free,
And the ocean wind is caressing me,
The wild wind from that wavy main
I never thought to see again.

Bless thee, Bright Sea – and glorious dome,
And my own world, my spirit's home;
Bless thee, bless all – I cannot speak;
My voice is choked, but not with grief;

And salt-drops from my haggard cheek
Descend, like rain upon the heath.

How long they've wet a dungeon floor,
Falling on flag-stones damp and grey!
I used to weep even in my sleep:
The night was dreadful, like the day.

I used to weep when winter's snow
Whirled through the grating stormily,
But then it was a calmer woe
For everything was drear as me.

The bitterest time, the worst of all,
Was that in which the summer sheen
Cast a green lustre on the wall
That told of fields of lovelier green.

Often I've sat down on the ground,
Gazing up to that flush scarce seen,
Till, heedless of the darkness round,
My soul has sought a land serene.

It sought the arch of heaven divine,
The pure blue heaven with clouds of gold;
It sought thy father's home and mine
As I remembered it of old.

O even now too horribly
Come back the feelings that would swell,
When with my face hid on my knee
I strove the bursting groans to quell.

I flung myself upon the stone,
I howled and tore my tangled hair,
And then, when the first gush had flown,
Lay in unspeakable despair.

Sometimes a curse, sometimes a prayer,
Would quiver on my parchéd tongue;
But both without a murmur there
Died in the breast from whence they sprung.

And so the day would fade on high,
And darkness quench that lonely beam,
And slumber mould my misery
Into some strange and spectral dream,
Whose fantom horrors made me know
The worst extent of human woe –

But this is past, and why return
O'er such a past to brood and mourn?
Shake off the fetters, break the chain,
And live and love and smile again.

The waste of youth, the waste of years,
Departed in that dongeon's thrall;
The gnawing grief, the hopeless tears,
Forget them, O forget them all!

7 August 1837

THE SUN HAS SET, AND THE LONG GRASS NOW

The sun has set, and the long grass now
Waves drearily in the evening wind;
And the wild bird has flown from that old grey stone,
In some warm nook a couch to find.

In all the lonely landscape round
I see no sight and hear no sound,
Except the wind that far away
Comes sighing o'er the heathy sea.

1837

WIND, SINK TO REST IN THE HEATHER

Wind, sink to rest in the heather,
Thy wild voice suits not me:
I would have dreary weather,
But all devoid of thee.

Sun, set from that evening heaven,
Thy glad smile wins not mine;
If light at all is given,
O give me Cynthia's shine.

1837

A SUDDEN CHASM OF GHASTLY LIGHT

A sudden chasm of ghastly light
Yawned in the city's reeling wall;
And a long thundering through the night
Proclaimed our triumph – Tyndarum's fall.

The shrieking wind sank mute and mild,
The smothering snow-clouds rolled away;
And cold – how cold! – wan moonlight smiled
Where those black ruins mouldering lay.

'Twas over – all the battle's madness,
The bursting fires, the cannons' roar,
The yells, the groans, the frenzied gladness,
The death, the danger, alarmed no more.

In plundered churches piled with dead
The heavy charger neighed for food;
The wounded soldier laid his head
'Neath roofless chambers splashed with blood.

I could not sleep: through that wild siege
My heart had fiercely burned and bounded;
The outward tumult seemed to assuage
The inward tempest it surrounded.

*   *   *   *   *

But dreams like this I cannot bear,
And silence whets the fang of pain;
I felt the full flood of despair
Returning to my breast again.

My couch lay in a ruined Hall
Whose windows looked on the minster-yard,
Where chill, chill whiteness covered all –
Both stone and urn and withered sward.

The shattered glass let in the air,
And with it came a wandering moan,
A sound unutterably drear
That made me shrink to be alone.

One black yew-tree grew just below –
I thought its boughs so sad might wail;
Their ghostly fingers, flecked with snow,
Rattled against an old vault's rail.

I listened – no; 'twas life that still
Lingered in some deserted heart;
O God! what caused the shuddering shrill,
That anguished, agonizing start?

An undefined, an awful dream,
A dream of what had been before;
A memory whose blighting beam
Was flitting o'er me evermore.

A frightful feeling, frenzy-born –
I hurried down the dark oak stair;
I reached the door whose hinges torn
Flung streaks of moonshine here and there.

I pondered not, I drew the bar:
An icy glory caught mine eye,
From that wide heaven where every star
Stared like a dying memory;

And there the great cathedral rose,
Discrowned, but most majestic so;
It looked down in serene repose
On its own realm of buried woe.

14 October 1837

THE OLD CHURCH TOWER AND
GARDEN WALL

The old church tower and garden wall
Are black with autumn rain,
And dreary winds foreboding call
The darkness down again.

I watched how evening took the place
Of glad and glorious day;
I watched a deeper gloom efface
The evening's lingering ray.

And as I gazed on the cheerless sky
Sad thoughts rose in my mind . . .

October 1837

FAR AWAY IS THE LAND OF REST

Far away is the land of rest;
Thousand miles are stretched between,
Many a mountain's stormy crest,
Many a desert void of green.

Wasted, worn is the traveller,
Dark his heart and dim his eye;
Without hope or comforter,
Faltering, faint, and ready to die.

Often he looks to the ruthless sky,
Often he looks o'er his dreary road;
Often he wishes down to lie
And render up life's tiresome load.

But yet faint not, mournful man;
Leagues on leagues are left behind
Since your sunless course began;
Then go on to toil resigned.

If you still despair control,
Hush its whispers in your breast;
You shall reach the final goal,
You shall win the land of rest.

October 1837

SLEEP BRINGS NO JOY

Sleep brings no joy to me,
Remembrance never dies;
My soul is given to misery
And lives in sighs.

Sleep brings no rest to me;
The shadows of the dead
My waking eyes may never see
Surround my bed.

Sleep brings no hope to me;
In soundest sleep they come,
And with their doleful imagery
Deepen the gloom.

Sleep brings no strength to me,
No power renewed to brave:
I only sail a wilder sea,
A darker wave.

Sleep brings no friend to me
To soothe and aid to bear;
They all gaze, oh, how scornfully,
And I despair.

Sleep brings no wish to knit
My harassed heart beneath:
My only wish is to forget
In the sleep of death.

November 1837

STRONG I STAND

Strong I stand, though I have borne
Anger, hate, and bitter scorn;
Strong I stand, and laugh to see
How mankind have fought with me.

Shade of mast'ry, I condemn
All the puny ways of men;
Free my heart, my spirit free;
Beckon, and I'll follow thee.

False and foolish mortal, know,
If you scorn the world's disdain,
Your mean soul is far below
Other worms, however vain.

Thing of dust, with boundless pride,
Dare you take me for a guide?
With the humble I will be:
Haughty men are nought to me.

I'LL COME WHEN THOU ART SADDEST

I'll come when thou art saddest,
Laid alone in the darkened room;
When the mad day's mirth has vanished,
And the smile of joy is banished
From evening's chilly gloom.

I'll come when the heart's real feeling
Has entire, unbiased sway,
And my influence o'er thee stealing,
Grief deepening, joy congealing,
Shall bear thy soul away.

Listen! 'tis just the hour,
The awful time for thee:
Dost thou not feel upon thy soul
A flood of strange sensations roll,
Forerunners of a sterner power,
Heralds of me?

November 1837

TO A WREATH OF SNOW

O transient voyager of heaven!
O silent sign of winter skies!
What adverse wind thy sail has driven
To dungeons where a prisoner lies?

Methinks the hands that shut the sun
So sternly from this mourning brow
Might still their rebel task have done
And checked a thing so frail as thou.

They would have done it had they known
The talisman that dwelt in thee,
For all the suns that ever shone
Have never been so kind to me.

For many a week, and many a day
My heart was weighed with sinking gloom,
When morning rose in mourning grey
And faintly lit my prison room;

But, angel-like, when I awoke,
Thy silvery form so soft and fair,
Shining through darkness, sweetly spoke
Of cloudy skies and mountains bare –

The dearest to a mountaineer,
Who all life long has loved the snow
That crowned her native summits drear,
Better than greenest plains below.

And, voiceless, soulless messenger,
Thy presence waked a thrilling tone
That comforts me while thou art here,
And will sustain when thou art gone.

December 1837

I'M HAPPIEST WHEN MOST AWAY

I'm happiest when most away
I can bear my soul from its home of clay
On a windy night when the moon is bright,
And the eye can wander through worlds of light, –

When I am not and none beside –
Nor earth nor sea nor cloudless sky –
But only spirit wandering wide
Through infinite immensity.

ALL HUSHED AND STILL WITHIN THE HOUSE

All hushed and still within the house;
Without – all wind and driving rain;
But something whispers to my mind
Through rain and through the wailing wind;
   Never again.
Never again? Why not again?
Memory has power as real as thine.

WEANED FROM LIFE AND TORN AWAY

Weaned from life and torn away
In the morning of thy day,
Bound in everlasting gloom,
Buried in a hopeless tomb.

Yet upon thy bended knee
Thank the power that banished thee;
Chain and bar and dongeon wall
Saved thee from a deadlier thrall.

Thank the power that made thee part
Ere that parting broke thy heart.

February 1838

HERE, WITH MY KNEE UPON THY STONE

Here, with my knee upon thy stone,
I bid adieu to feelings gone;
I leave with thee my tears and pain,
And rush into the world again.

1838

THIS SHALL BE THY LULLABY

This shall be thy lullaby
Rocking on the stormy sea,
Though it roar in thunder wild
Sleep, stilly sleep, my dark haired child.

When our shuddering boat was crossing
Elderno lake so rudely tossing
Than 'twas first my nursling smiled;
Sleep, softly sleep, my fair browed child.

Waves about thy cradle break,
Foamy tears are on thy cheek
Yet the Ocean's self grows mild
When it bears my slumbering child.

May 1838

THERE ARE TWO TREES IN A LONELY FIELD

There are two trees in a lonely field;
They breathe a spell to me;
A dreary thought their dark boughs yield,
All waving solemnly.

June 1838

'TWAS ONE OF THOSE
DARK, CLOUDY DAYS

'Twas one of those dark, cloudy days
That sometimes come in summer's blaze,
When heaven drops not, when earth is still,
And deeper green is on the hill.

June 1838

WHAT IS THAT SMOKE
THAT EVER STILL

What is that smoke that ever still
Comes rolling down that dark brown hill?

OLD HALL OF ELBË

Old Hall of Elbë, ruined, lonely now:
House to which the voice of life shall never more
    return;
Chambers roofless, desolate, where weeds and ivy
    grow;
Windows through whose broken arches the night-
    winds sadly mourn;
Home of the departed, the long-departed dead.

GLENEDEN'S DREAM

Tell me, watcher, is it winter?
Say how long my sleep has been?
Have the woods, I left so lovely,
Lost their robes of tender green?

Is the morning slow in coming?
Is the night-time loath to go?
Tell me, are the dreary mountains
Drearier still with drifted snow?

'Captive, since thou sawest the forest,
'All its leaves have died away
'And another March has woven
'Garlands for another May.

'Ice has barred the Arctic water,
'Soft south winds have set it free;
'And once more to deep green valley
'Golden flowers might welcome thee.'

Watcher, in this lonely prison,
Shut from joy and kindly air,
Heaven, descending in a vision,
Taught my soul to do and bear.

It was a night, a night of winter;
I lay on the dungeon floor,
And all other sounds were silent –
All, except the river's roar.

Over Death, and Desolation,
Fireless hearths and lifeless homes;
Over orphans' heart-sick sorrows,
. . . fathers' bloody tombs;

Over friends that my arms never
Might embrace, in love again –
Memory pondered, until madness
Struck its poignard in my brain.

Deepest slumber followed raving,
Yet, methought, I brooded still;
Still I saw my country bleeding,
Dying for a Tyrant's will. –

Not because *my* bliss was blasted,
Burned within the avenging flame;
Not because my scattered kindred
Died in woe, or lived in shame.

God doth know, I would have given
Every bosom dear to me,
Could that sacrifice have purchased
Tortured Gondal's liberty!

But, that at Ambition's bidding
All her cherished hopes should wane;
That her noblest sons should muster,
Strive, and fight and fall in vain –

Hut and castle, hall and cottage,
Roofless, crumbling to the ground –
Mighty Heaven, a glad Avenger
Thy eternal justice found!

Yes, the arm that once would shudder
Even to pierce a wounded deer,
I beheld it, unrelenting,
Choke in blood its sovereign's prayer.

Glorious dream! I saw the city
Blazing in imperial shine;
And among adoring thousands
Stood a man of form divine.

None need point the princely victim –
Now he smiles with royal pride!
Now his glance is bright as lightning:
Now – the knife is in his side!

Ha, I saw how death could darken –
Darken that triumphant eye!
His red heart's blood drenched my dagger;
My ear drank his dying sigh!

Shadows come! What means this midnight?
O my God, I know it all!
Know the fever-dream is over!
Unavenged the Avenger's fall!

21 May 1838

IN DUNGEONS DARK

In dungeons dark I cannot sing,
In sorrow's thrall 'tis hard to smile:
What bird can soar with broken wing?
What heart can bleed and joy the while?
1838

FALL, LEAVES, FALL

Fall, leaves, fall; die, flowers, away;
Lengthen night and shorten day.
Every leaf speaks bliss to me
Fluttering from the autumn tree.
I shall smile when wreaths of snow
Blossom where the rose should grow;
I shall sing when night's decay
Ushers in a drearier day.
1838

THE MOON IS SHINING

Geraldine, the moon is shining
With so soft, so bright a ray;
Seems it not that eve, declining,
Ushered in a fairer day?

While the wind is whispering only,
Far across the water borne,
Let us in this silence lonely
Sit beneath the ancient thorn.

Wild the road, and rough and dreary;
Barren all the moorland round;
Rude the couch that rests us weary;
Mossy stone and heathy ground.

But when winter storms were meeting
In the moonless midnight dome
Did we heed the tempest's beating,
Howling round our spirits' home?

No, that tree, with branches riven
Whitening in the whirl of snow,
As it tossed against the heaven
Sheltered happy hearts below –

And at Autumn's mild returning
Shall our feet forget that way?
And in Cynthia's silver morning,
Geraldine, wilt thou delay?

17 October 1838

TO SAY THE WORD ADIEU

I knew not 'twas so dire a crime
To say the word, Adieu;
But this shall be the only time
My slighted heart shall sue.

The wild moorside, the winter morn,
The gnarled and ancient tree –
If in your breast they waken scorn,
Shall wake the same in me.

I can forget black eyes and brows
And lips of rosy charm
If you forget the sacred vows
Those faithless lips could form.

If hard commands can tame your love,
Or prison walls can hold
I would not wish to grieve above
A thing so false and cold.

And there are bosoms bound to mine
With links both tried and strong;
And there are eyes, whose lightning shine
Has warmed and blessed me long:

Those eyes shall make my only day,
Shall set my spirit free
And chase the foolish thoughts away
That mourn your memory!

17 October 1838

LIGHT UP THY HALLS

Light up thy halls! 'Tis closing day;
I'm drear and lone and far away –
Cold blows on my breast the northwind's bitter sigh,
And oh, my couch is bleak beneath the rainy sky!

Light up thy halls – and think not of me;
That face is absent now thou hast hated so to see –
Bright be thine eyes, undimmed their dazzling shine,
For never, never more shall they encounter mine!

The desert moor is dark; there is tempest in the air;
I have breathed my only wish in one last, one burning
    prayer –
A prayer that would come forth although it lingered
    long;
That set on fire my heart, but froze upon my tongue.

And now, it shall be done before the morning rise:
I will not watch the sun ascend in yonder skies.
One task alone remains – thy pictured face to view –
And then I grow to prove if God, at least, be true!

Do I not see thee now? Thy black resplendent hair;
Thy glory-beaming brow, and smile how heavenly fair!
Thine eyes are turned away – those eyes I would not see:
Their dark, their deadly ray would more than
    madden me.

There, go, Deceiver, go! My hand is streaming wet;
My heart's blood flows to buy the blessing – To forget!
Oh could that lost heart give back, back again to thine,
One tenth part of the pain that clouds my dark decline!

Oh could I see thy lids weighed down in cheerless woe;
Too full to hide their tears, too stern to overflow;
Oh could I know thy soul with equal grief was torn,
This fate might be endured – this anguish might be
    borne!

How gloomy grows the night! 'Tis Gondal's wind that
    blows;
I shall not tread again the deep glens where it rose –
I feel it on my face – 'Where, wild blast, dost thou
    roam?
'What do we, wanderer, here, so far away from home?

'I do not need thy breath to cool my death-cold brow;
'But go to that far land, where she is shining now;
'Tell her my latest wish, tell her my dreary doom;
'Say, that *my* pangs are past, but *hers* are yet to come.'

Vain words, vain frenzied thoughts! No ear can hear
    me call –
Lost in the vacant air my frantic curses fall –
And could she see me now, perchance her lip would
    smile,
Would smile in careless pride and utter scorn the
    while!

And yet, for all her hate, each parting glance would tell
A stronger passion breathed, burned in this last fare-
    well.
Unconquered in my soul the Tyrant rules me still –
Life bows to my control, but *Love* I cannot kill!

1 November 1838

THE STARRY NIGHT SHALL TIDINGS BRING

The starry night shall tidings bring:
Go out upon the breezy moor,
Watch for a bird with sable wing,
And beak and talons dropping gore.

Look not around, look not beneath,
But mutely trace its airy way;
Mark where it lights upon the heath;
Then wanderer kneel thee down and pray.

What fortune may await thee there
I will not and I dare not tell;
But Heaven is moved by fervent prayer,
And God is mercy – fare thee well!

November 1838

LOUD WITHOUT THE WIND WAS ROARING

Loud without the wind was roaring
Through the waned autumnal sky,
Drenching wet, the cold rain pouring
Spoke of stormy winters nigh.

All too like that dreary eve
Sighed within repining grief –
Sighed at first – but sighed not long
Sweet – How softly sweet it came!
Wild words of an ancient song,
Undefined, without a name.

'It was spring, for the skylark was singing.'
Those words they awakened a spell –
They unlocked a deep fountain whose springing
Nor Absence nor Distance can quell.

In the gloom of a cloudy November
They uttered the music of May –
They kindled the perishing ember
Into fervour that could not decay.

Awaken on all my dear moorlands
The wind in its glory and pride!
O call me from valleys and highlands
To walk by the hill-river's side!

It is swelled with the first snowy weather;
The rocks they are icy and hoar
And darker waves round the long heather
And the fern-leaves are sunny no more.

There are no yellow-stars on the mountain,
The blue-bells have long died away
From the brink at the moss-bedded fountain,
From the side of the wintery brae –

But lovelier than cornfields all waving
In emerald and scarlet and gold
Are the slopes where the north-wind is raving,
And the glens where I wandered of old.

'It was morning, the bright sun was beaming.'
How sweetly that brought back to me
The time when nor labour nor dreaming
Broke the sleep of the happy and free!

But blithely we rose as the dusk heaven
Was melting to amber and blue
And swift were the wings to our feet given
While we traversed the meadows of dew.

For the moors, for the moors where the short grass
Like velvet beneath us should lie!
For the moors, for the moors where each high pass
Rose sunny against the clear sky!

For the moors, where the linnet was trilling
Its song on the old granite stone –
Where the lark – the wild sky-lark was filling
Every breast with delight like its own.

What language can utter the feeling
That rose when, in exile afar,
On the brow of a lonely hill kneeling
I saw the brown heath growing there.

It was scattered and stunted, and told me
That soon even that would be gone.
It whispered: 'The grim walls enfold me;
'I have bloomed in my last summer's sun.'

But not the loved music whose waking
Makes the soul of the Swiss die away
Has a spell more adored and heart-breaking
Than in its half-blighted bells lay –

The spirit that bent 'neath its power
How it longed, how it burned to be free!
If I could have wept in that hour
Those tears had been heaven to me.

Well, well, the sad minutes are moving
Though loaded with trouble and pain;
And sometime the loved and the loving
Shall meet on the mountains again.

11 November 1838

A LITTLE WHILE, A LITTLE WHILE

A little while, a little while
The noisy crowd are barred away;
And I can sing and I can smile –
A little while I've holyday!

Where wilt thou go, my harassed heart?
Full many a land invites thee now;
And places near, and far apart
Have rest for thee, my weary brow.

There is a spot 'mid barren hills
Where winter howls and driving rain,
But if the dreary tempest chills
There is a light that warms again.

The house is old, the trees are bare
And moonless bends the misty dome
But what on earth is half so dear –
So longed for as the hearth of home?

The mute bird sitting on the stone,
The dank moss dripping from the wall,
The garden-walk with weeds o'ergrown
I love them – how I love them all!

Shall I go there? or shall I seek
Another clime, another sky,
Where tongues familiar music speak
In accents dear to memory?

Yes, as I mused, the naked room,
The flickering firelight died away
And from the midst of cheerless gloom
I passed to bright, unclouded day –

A little and a lone green lane
That opened on a common wide
A distant, dreamy, dim blue chain
Of mountains circling every side –

A heaven so clear, an earth so calm,
So sweet, so soft, so hushed an air
And, deepening still the dream-like charm,
Wild moor-sheep feeding everywhere.

That was the scene – I knew it well,
I knew the path-ways far and near
That winding o'er each billowy swell
Marked out the tracks of wandering deer.

Could I have lingered but an hour
It well had paid a week of toil,
But truth has banished fancy's power
I hear my dungeon bars recoil –

Even as I stood with upturned eye
Absorbed in bliss so deep and clear
My hour of rest had fleeted by
And given me back to weary care.

4 December 1838

HOW STILL, HOW HAPPY!

How still, how happy! Those are words
That once would scarce agree together
I loved the plashing of the surge –
The changing heaven the breezy weather

More than smooth seas and cloudless skies
And solemn, soothing, softened airs
That in the forest woke no sighs
And from the green spray shook no tears.

How still, how happy! Now I feel
Where silence dwells is sweeter far
Than laughing mirth's most joyous swell
However pure its raptures are.

Come, sit down on this sunny stone:
'Tis wintry light o'er flowerless moors –
But sit – for we are all alone
And clear expand heaven's breathless shores.

I could think in the withered grass
Spring's budding wreaths we might discern;
The violet's eye might shyly flash
And young leaves shoot among the fern.

It is but thought – full many a night
The snow shall clothe these hills afar
And storms shall add a drearier blight
And winds shall wage a wilder war

Before the lark may herald in
Fresh foliage twined with blossoms fair
And summer days again begin
Their glory-haloed crown to wear.

Yet my heart loves December's smile
As much as July's beam:
Then let us sit and watch the while
The blue ice curdling on the stream.

7 December 1838

FROM OUR EVENING FIRESIDE

From our evening fireside now,
Merry laugh and cheerful tone,
Smiling eye and cloudless brow,
Mirth and music, all are flown:

Yet the grass before the door
Grows as green in April rain;
And as blithely as of yore
Larks have poured their day-long strain.

Is it fear, or is it sorrow
Checks the stagnant stream of joy?
Do we tremble that tomorrow
May our present peace destroy?

For past misery are we weeping?
What is past can hurt no more;
And the gracious heavens are keeping
Aid for that which lies before.

One is absent, and for one
Cheerless, chill is our hearthstone.
One is absent, and for him
Cheeks are pale and eyes are dim.

Arthur, brother, Gondal's shore
Rested from the battle's roar –
Arthur, brother, we returned
Back to Desmond lost and mourned.

Thou didst purchase by thy fall
Home for us and peace for all;
Yet, how darkly dawned that day –
Dreadful was the price to pay!

Just as once, through sun and mist
I have climbed the mountain's breast,
Still my gun with certain aim
Brought to earth the fluttering game.

But the very dogs repined
Though I called with whistle shrill,
Listlessly they lagged behind,
Looking backward o'er the hill.

Sorrow was not vocal there:
Mute their pain and my despair;
But the joy of life was flown:
He was gone, and we were lone.

So it is by morn and eve –
So it is in field and hall –
For the absent one we grieve,
One being absent saddens All.

17 April 1839

I KNOW NOT HOW IT FALLS ON ME

I know not how it falls on me,
This summer evening, hushed and lone;
Yet the faint wind comes soothingly
With something of an olden tone.

Forgive me if I've shunned so long
Your gentle greeting, earth and air!
But sorrow withers even the strong,
And who can fight against despair?

8 June 1839

LINES

The soft unclouded blue of air,
The earth as golden-green and fair
And bright as Eden's used to be:
That air and earth have rested me.

Laid on the grass I lapsed away,
Sank back again to childhood's day;
All harsh thoughts perished, memory mild
Subdued both grief and passion wild.

But did the sunshine even now
That bathed his stern and swarthy brow,
Oh, did it wake – I long to know –
One whisper, one sweet dream in him,
One lingering joy that years ago
Had faded – lost in distance dim?

That iron man was born like me,
And he was once an ardent boy:
He must have felt, in infancy,
The glory of a summer sky.

Though storms untold his mind have tossed,
He cannot utterly have lost
Remembrance of his early home –
So lost that not a gleam may come;

No vision of his mother's face
When she so fondly would set free
Her darling child from her embrace
To roam till eve at liberty:

Nor of his haunts, nor of the flowers
His tiny hand would grateful bear
Returning from the darkening bowers,
To weave into her glossy hair.

I saw the light breeze kiss his cheek,
His fingers 'mid the roses twined;
I watched to mark one transient streak
Of pensive softness shade his mind.

The open window showed around
A glowing park and glorious sky,
And thick woods swelling with the sound
Of Nature's mingled harmony.

Silent he sat. That stormy breast
At length, I said, has deigned to rest;
At length above that spirit flows
The waveless ocean of repose.

Let me draw near: 'twill soothe to view
His dark eyes dimmed with holy dew;
Remorse even now may wake within,
And half unchain his soul from sin.

Perhaps this is the destined hour
When Hell shall lose its fatal power
And Heaven itself shall bend above,
To hail the soul redeemed by love.

Unmarked I gazed; my idle thought
Passed with the ray whose shine it caught;
One glance revealed how little care
He felt for all the beauty there.

Oh, crime can make the heart grow old
Sooner than years of wearing woe;
Can turn the warmest bosom cold
As winter wind or polar snow.

28 April 1839

TO THE BLUEBELL

Sacred watcher, wave thy bells!
Fair hill flower and woodland child!
Dear to me in deep green dells –
Dearest on the mountains wild.

Bluebell, even as all divine
I have seen my darling shine –
Bluebell, even as wan and frail
I have seen my darling fail –
Lift thy head and speak to me,
Soothing thoughts are breathed by thee.

Thus they murmur, 'Summer's sun
'Warms me till my life is done.
'Would I rather choose to die
'Under winter's ruthless sky?

'Glad I bloom and calm I fade;
'Weeping twilight dews my bed;
'Mourner, mourner, dry thy tears –
'Sorrow comes with lengthened years!'

9 May 1839

MAY FLOWERS ARE OPENING

May flowers are opening
And leaves unfolding free;
There are bees in every blossom,
And birds on every tree.

The sun is gladly shining,
The stream sings merrily,
And I only am pining,
And all is dark to me.

O cold, cold is my heart!
It will not, cannot rise;
It feels no sympathy
With those refulgent skies.

Dead, dead is my joy,
I long to be at rest;
I wished the damp earth covered
This desolate breast.

If I were quite alone,
It might not be so drear
When all hope was gone;
At least I could not fear.

But the glad eyes around me
Must weep as mine have done,
And I must see the same gloom
Eclipse their morning sun.

If heaven would rain on me
That future storm of care,
So their fond hearts were free,
I'd be content to bear.

Alas! as lightning withers
The young and aged tree,
Both they and I shall fall beneath
The fate we cannot flee.

25 May 1839

AND NOW THE HOUSE-DOG
STRETCHED ONCE MORE

And now the house-dog stretched once more
His limbs upon the glowing floor;
The children half resumed their play,
Though from the warm hearth scared away.
The good-wife left her spinning-wheel,
And spread with smiles the evening meal;
The shepherd placed a seat and pressed
To their poor fare his unknown guest.
And he unclasped his mantle now,
And raised the covering from his brow;
Said, 'Voyagers by land and sea
'Were seldom feasted daintily';
And checked his host by adding stern
He'd no refinement to unlearn.
A silence settled on the room;
The cheerful welcome sank to gloom;
But not these words, though cold and high,
So froze their hospitable joy.
No – there was something in his face,
Some nameless thing they could not trace,
And something in his voice's tone
Which turned their blood as chill as stone.
The ringlets of his long black hair
Fell o'er a cheek most ghastly fair.
Youthful he seemed – but worn as they
Who spend too soon their youthful day.
When his glance drooped, 'twas hard to quell
Unbidden feelings' sudden swell;
And pity scarce her tears could hide,
So sweet that brow, with all its pride;
But when upraised his eye would dart
An icy shudder through the heart.

Compassion changed to horror then
And fear to meet that gaze again.
It was not hatred's tiger-glare,
Nor the wild anguish of despair;
It was not useless misery
Which mocks at friendship's sympathy.
No – lightning all unearthly shone
Deep in that dark eye's circling zone,
Such withering lightning as we deem
None but a spectre's look may beam;
And glad they were when he turned away
And wrapped him in his mantle grey,
Leant down his head upon his arm
And veiled from view their basilisk charm.

12 July 1839

THOU STANDEST IN THE GREENWOOD NOW

'Thou standest in the greenwood now
'The place, the hour the same –
'And here the fresh leaves gleam and glow
'And there, down in the lake below,
'The tiny ripples flame.

'The breeze sings like a summer breeze
'Should sing in summer skies
'And tower-like rocks and tent-like trees
'In mingled glory rise.

'But where is he today, today?'
'O question not with me.'
'I will not, Lady, only say
'Where may thy lover be?

'Is he upon some distant shore
'Or is he on the sea
'Or is the heart thou dost adore,
'A faithless heart to thee?'

'The heart I love, whate'er betide,
'Is faithful as the grave,
'And neither foreign lands divide
'Nor yet the rolling wave.'

'Then why should sorrow cloud that brow
'And tears those eyes bedim?
'Reply this once – is it that thou
'Hast faithless been to him?'

'I gazed upon the cloudless moon
'And loved her all the night
'Till morning came and ardent noon,
'Then I forgot her light –

'No – not forgot, eternally
'Remains its memory dear;
'But could the day seem dark to me
'Because the night was fair?

'I well may mourn that only one
'Can light my future sky,
'Even though by such a radiant sun
'My moon of life must die.'

SHED NO TEARS O'ER THAT TOMB

Shed no tears o'er that tomb
For there are Angels weeping;
Mourn not him whose doom
Heaven itself is mourning.
Look how in sable gloom
The clouds are earthward sweeping,
And earth receives them home,
Even darker clouds returning.

Is it when good men die
That sorrow wakes above?
Grieve saints when other spirits fly
To swell their choir of love?

Ah no, with louder sound
The golden harp-strings quiver
When good men gain the happy ground
Where they must dwell for ever.

But he who slumbers there,
His bark will strive no more
Across the waters of despair
To reach that glorious shore.

The time of grace is past
And mercy scorned and tried
Forsakes to utter wrath at last
The soul so steeled by pride.

That wrath will never spare,
Will never pity know,
Will mock its victim's maddened prayer,
Will triumph in his woe.

Shut from his Maker's smile
The accursed man shall be:
For mercy reigns a little while,
But hate eternally.

26 July 1839

SLEEP NOT, DREAM NOT

Sleep not, dream not – this bright day
Will not, cannot last for aye;
Bliss like thine is bought by years
Dark with torment and with tears.

Sweeter far than placid pleasure,
Purer, higher beyond measure –
Yet alas the sooner turning
Into hopeless, endless mourning.

I love thee, boy; for all divine,
All full of God thy features shine.
Darling enthusiast, holy child,
Too good for this world's warring wild,
Too heavenly now but doomed to be
Hell-like in heart and misery.

And what shall change that angel-brow,
And quench that spirit's glorious glow?
Relentless laws that disallow
True virtue and true joy below.

And blame me not if when the dread
Of suffering clouds thy youthful head,
If when by crime and sorrow tost
Thy wandering bark is wrecked and lost

I too depart, I too decline,
And make thy path no longer mine.
'Tis thus that human minds will turn,
All doomed alike to sin and mourn –
Yet all with long gaze fixed afar,
Adoring virtue's distant star.

HOW LONG WILL YOU REMAIN?

How long will you remain? The midnight hour
Has tolled the last note from the minster tower.
Come, come: the fire is dead, the lamp burns low,
Your eyelids droop, a weight is on your brow.
Your cold hands hardly hold the useless pen;
Come: morn will give recovered strength again.

'No: let me linger; leave me, let me be
'A little longer in this reverie.
'I'm happy now, and would you tear away
'My blissful dream, that never comes with day:
'A vision dear, though false, for well my mind
'Knows what a bitter waking waits behind?'

'Can there be pleasure in this shadowy room,
'With windows yawning on intenser gloom,
'And such a dreary wind so bleakly sweeping
''Round walls where only you are vigil keeping?
'Besides, your face has not a sign of joy;
'And more than tearful sorrow fills your eye.
'Look on those woods, look on that heaven lorn,
'And think how changed they'll be tomorrow morn:
'The dome of heaven expanding bright and blue,
'The leaves, the green grass, sprinkled thick with dew,
'The wet mists rising on the river's breast,
'And wild birds bursting from their songless nest,
'And your own children's merry voices chasing
'The fancies grief, not pleasure, has been tracing.'

'Ay, speak of these; but can you tell me why
'Day breathes such beauty over earth and sky,
'And waking sounds revive, restore again
'The hearts that all night long have throbbed in pain?

'Is it not that the sunshine and the wind
'Lure from its self the mourner's woe-worn mind;
'And all the joyous music breathing by,
'And all the splendour of that cloudless sky,
'Re-give him shadowy gleams of infancy,
'And draw his tired gaze from futurity?'

12 August 1839

FAIR SINKS THE SUMMER EVENING NOW

Fair sinks the summer evening now
In softened glory round my home;
The sky upon its holy brow
Wears not a cloud that speaks of gloom.

The old tower, shrined in golden light,
Looks down on the descending sun –
So gently evening blends with night,
You scarce can say that day is done.

And this is just the joyous hour
When we were wont to burst away,
To 'scape from labour's tyrant power
And cheerfully go out to play.

Then why is all so sad and lone?
No merry foot-step on the stair –
No laugh – no heart-awaking tone,
But voiceless silence everywhere.

I've wandered round our garden-ground,
And still it seemed, at every turn,
That I should greet approaching feet,
And words upon the breezes borne.

In vain – they will not come today,
And morning's beam will rise as drear.
Then tell me – are they gone for aye?
Our sun blinks through the mists of care.

Ah no, reproving Hope doth say,
Departed joys 'tis fond to mourn,
When every storm that hides their ray
Prepares a more divine return.

30 August 1839

BETWEEN DISTRESS AND PLEASURE

O between distress and pleasure
Fond affection cannot be!
Wretched hearts in vain would treasure
Friendship's joys when others flee.

Well I know thine eye would never
Smile, while mine grieved, willingly;
Yet I know thine eye for ever
Could not weep in sympathy.

Let us part, the time is over
When I thought and felt like thee;
I will be an Ocean rover,
I will sail the desert sea.

Isles there are beyond its billow:
Lands where woe may wander free;
And, beloved, thy midnight pillow
Will be soft unwatched by me.

Not on each returning morrow,
When thy heart bounds ardently,
Need'st thou then dissemble sorrow,
Marking my despondency.

Day by day some dreary token
Will forsake thy memory
Till at last all old links broken
I shall be a dream to thee.

15 October 1839

THERE WAS A TIME WHEN MY CHEEK BURNED

There was a time when my cheek burned
To give such scornful fiends the lie;
Ungoverned nature madly spurned
The law that bade it not defy.
O in the days of ardent youth
I would have given my life for truth.

For truth, for right, for liberty,
I would have gladly, freely died;
And now I calmly hear and see
The vain man smile, the fool deride;
Though not because my heart is tame,
Though not for fear, though not for shame.

My soul chafes at every tone
Of selfish and self-blinded error;
My breast still braves the world alone,
Steeled as it ever was to terror;
Only I know, however I frown.
The same world will go rolling on.

October 1839

THE WIND I HEAR IT SIGHING

The wind I hear it sighing
With Autumn's saddest sound –
Withered leaves as thick are lying
As spring-flowers on the ground.

This dark night has won me
To wander far away –
Old feelings gather fast upon me
Like vultures round their prey.

Kind were they once, and cherished,
But cold and cheerless now –
I would their lingering shades had perished
When their light left my brow.

'Tis like old age pretending
The softness of a child,
My altered hardened spirit bending
To meet their fancies wild.

Yet could I with past pleasures
Past woe's oblivion buy,
That by the death of my dearest treasures
My deadliest pains might die.

O then another daybreak
Might haply dawn above –
Another summer gild my cheek,
My soul, another love.

29 October 1839 (or 1838)

EMILY BRONTË

LOVE AND FRIENDSHIP

Love is like the wild rose-briar,
Friendship like the holly-tree –
The holly is dark when the rose-briar blooms
But which will bloom most constantly?

The wild rose-briar is sweet in spring,
Its summer blossoms scent the air
Yet wait till winter comes again
And who will call the wild-briar fair?

Then scorn the silly rose-wreath now
And deck thee with the holly's sheen,
That when December blights thy brow
He still may leave thy garland green.

THERE SHOULD BE NO DESPAIR FOR YOU

There should be no despair for you
While nightly stars are burning –
While evening sheds its silent dew
Or sunshine gilds the morning.

There should be no despair – though tears
May flow down like a river –
Are not the best beloved of years
Around your heart for ever?

They weep – you weep. It must be so –
Winds sigh as you are sighing,
And Winter pours its grief in snow
Where Autumn's leaves are lying.

– They revive and from their fate
Your fate cannot be parted:
Then journey onward not elate
But *never* broken-hearted.

WELL, SOME MAY HATE
AND SOME MAY SCORN

'Well, some may hate and some may scorn
'And some may quite forget thy name
'But my sad heart must ever mourn
'Thy ruined hopes, thy blighted fame.'

'Twas thus I thought an hour ago
Even weeping o'er that wretch's woe.
One word turned back my gushing tears
And lit my altered eye with sneers.

'Then bless the friendly dust', I said,
'That hides thy unlamented head.
'Vain as thou wert, and weak as vain,
'The slave of falsehood, pride and pain,
'My heart has nought akin to thine –
'Thy soul is powerless over mine.'

But these were thoughts that vanished too –
Unwise, unholy and untrue –
Do I despise the timid deer
Because his limbs are fleet with fear?

Or would I mock the wolf's death-howl
Because his form is gaunt and foul?
Or hear with joy the leveret's cry
Because it cannot bravely die?

No – then above his memory
Let pity's heart as tender be:
Say 'Earth, lie lightly on that breast,
'And kind Heaven, grant that spirit rest!'

14 November 1839

HIS LAND MAY BURST
THE GALLING CHAIN

His land may burst the galling chain;
His people may be free again;
For them a thousand hopes remain,
But hope is dead for him.
Soft falls the moonlight on the sea,
Whose wild waves play at liberty,
And Gondal's wind sings solemnly
Its native midnight hymn.

Around his prison-walls it sings,
His heart is stirred through all its strings,
Because that sound remembrance brings
Of scenes that once have been.
His soul has left the storm below,
And reached a realm of sunless snow:
The region of unchanging woe,
Made voiceless by despair.

And Gerald's land may burst its chain,
His subjects may be free again;
For them a thousand hopes remain,
But hope is dead for him.
Set his sun of liberty;
Fixed is his earthly destiny;
A few years of captivity,
And then a captive's tomb.

START NOT! UPON THE MINSTER-WALL

Start not! upon the minster-wall
Sunshine is shed in holy calm;
And, lonely though my footsteps fall,
The saint shall shelter thee from harm.

Shrink not if it be summer noon –
This shadow should night's welcome be.
These stairs are steep, but landed soon
We'll rest us long and quietly.

What though our path be o'er the dead?
They slumber soundly in the tomb;
And why should mortals fear to tread
The pathway to their future home?

THAT DREARY LAKE,
THAT MIDNIGHT SKY

That dreary lake, that midnight sky,
That wan moon struggling through the cloud;
That sullen murmur, whispering by,
As if it dared not speak aloud,
Fall on my heart so sadly now
Wither my joy so lonely . . .

Touch them not, they bloom and smile,
But their roots are withering all the while.
Ah

I GAZED WITHIN THINE
EARNEST EYES

I gazed within thine earnest eyes,
And read the sorrow brooding there;
I saw thy young breast heave with sighs,
And envied such despair.

Go to the grave in youth's first woe!
That doom was written long ago.

EMILY BRONTË

IN PRISON

Thy sun is near meridian height
And my sun sinks in endless night;
But if that night bring only sleep
Then I shall rest, when thou wilt weep.

And say not, that my early tomb
Will give me to a darker doom.
Shall these long agonizing years
Be punished by eternal tears?

No, *that* I feel can never be;
A God of *hate* could hardly bear
To watch, through all eternity,
His own creation's dread despair!

The pangs that wring my mortal breast
Must claim from Justice lasting rest:
Enough, that this despairing breath
Will pass in anguish worse than death.

If I have sinned, long, long ago
That sin was purified by woe –
I've suffered on through night and day;
I've trod a dark and frightful way.

Earth's wilderness was round me spread;
Heaven's tempests beat my naked head.
I did not kneel – in vain would prayer
Have sought one gleam of mercy there!

How could I ask for pitying love
When that grim concave frowned above,
Hoarding its lightnings to destroy
My only and my priceless joy?

They struck – and long may Eden shine
Ere I would call its glories mine:
All Heaven's undreamt felicity
Could never blot the past from me.

No, years may cloud and death may sever
But what is done is done for ever –
And thou, false friend, and treacherous guide,
Go sate thy cruel heart with pride –

Go, load my memory with shame;
Speak but to curse my hated name;
My tortured limbs in dungeons bind
And spare my life to kill my mind.

Leave me in chains and darkness now
And when my very soul is worn;
When reason's light has left my brow
And madness cannot feel thy scorn;

Then come again – thou wilt not shrink;
I know thy soul is free from fear –
The last cup full of triumph drink,
Before the blank of death be there.

Thy raving, dying victim see;
Lost, cursed, degraded all for thee!
Gaze on the wretch – recall to mind
His golden days left long behind.

Does memory sleep in Lethean rest?
Or wakes its whisper in thy breast?
O Memory, wake! let scenes return
That even her haughty heart must mourn!

Reveal, where o'er a lone green wood
The moon of summer pours
Far down from heaven, its silver flood
On deep Elderno's shores –

There, lingering in the wild embrace
Youth's warm affections gave
She sits, and fondly seems to trace
His features in the wave.

And while on that reflected face
Her eyes intently dwell:
'Fernando, sing tonight,' she says,
'The lays I love so well.'

He smiles and sings though every air
Betrays the faith of yesterday;
His soul is glad to cast for her
Virtue and faith and Heaven away.

Well, thou hast paid me back my love!
But, if there be a God above
Whose arm is strong, whose word is true,
This hell shall wring thy spirit too!

6 January 1840

FAR, FAR AWAY IS MIRTH WITHDRAWN

Far, far away is mirth withdrawn;
'Tis three long hours before the morn
And I watch lonely, drearily –
So come, thou shade, commune with me.

Deserted one! thy corpse lies cold,
And mingled with a foreign mould.
Year after year the grass grows green
Above the dust where thou hast been.

I will not name thy blighted name
Tarnished by unforgotten shame;
Though not because my bosom torn
Joins the mad world in all its scorn.

Thy phantom face is dark with woe;
Tears have left ghastly traces there:
Those ceaseless tears! I wish their flow
Could quench thy wild despair.

They deluge my heart like the rain
On cursed Gomorrah's howling plain –
Yet when I hear thy foes deride
I must cling closely to thy side.

Our mutual foes – they will not rest
From trampling on thy buried breast;
Glutting their hatred with the doom
They picture thine, beyond the tomb.

But God is not like human-kind;
Man cannot read the Almighty mind;
Vengeance will never torture thee,
Nor hunt thy soul eternally.

Then do not in this night of grief,
This time of overwhelming fear,
O do not think that God can leave,
Forget, forsake, refuse to hear!

What have I dreamt? He lies asleep
With whom my heart would vainly weep:
He rests, and *I* endure the woe
That left his spirit long ago.

March 1840

AT SUCH A TIME

At such a time, in such a spot
The world seems made of light;
Our blissful hearts remember not
How surely follows night.

I cannot, Alfred, dream of aught
That casts a shade of woe;
That heaven is reigning in my thought
Which wood and wave and earth have caught
From skies that overflow.

That heaven which my sweet lover's brow
Has won me to adore,
Which from his blue eyes beaming now
Reflects a still intenser glow
Than Nature's heaven can pour.

I know our souls are all divine;
I know that when we die,
What seems the vilest, even like thine
A part of God himself shall shine
In perfect purity.

But coldly breaks November's day;
Its changes charmless all
Unmarked, unloved, they pass away;
We do not wish one hour to stay
Nor sigh at evening's fall.

And glorious is the gladsome rise
Of June's rejoicing morn;
And who with unregretful eyes
Can watch the lustre leave its skies
To twilight's shade forlorn?

Then art thou not my golden June;
All mist and tempest-free?
As shines earth's sun in summer noon
So heaven's sun shines in thee.

Let others seek its beams divine
In cell and cloister drear;
But I have found a fairer shrine
And happier worship here.

By dismal rites they win their bliss –
By penance, fasts, and fears.
I have one rite – a gentle kiss;
One penance – tender tears.

O could it thus for ever be
That I might so adore;
I'd ask for all eternity
To make a paradise for me,
My love – and nothing more!

6 May 1840
28 July 1843

IF GRIEF FOR GRIEF
CAN TOUCH THEE

If grief for grief can touch thee,
If answering woe for woe,
If any ruth can melt thee,
Come to me now!

I cannot be more lonely,
More drear I cannot be!
My worn heart throbs so wildly
'Twill break for thee.

And when the world despises –
When heaven repels my prayer,
Will not mine angel comfort?
Mine idol hear?

Yes by the tears I've poured,
By all my hours of pain,
O I shall surely win thee
Beloved, again!

18 May 1840

THE NIGHT WIND

In summer's mellow midnight
A cloudless moon shone through
Our open parlour window
And rosetrees wet with dew.

I sat in silent musing –
The soft wind waved my hair
It told me Heaven was glorious
And sleeping Earth was fair.

I needed not its breathing
To bring such thoughts to me
But still it whispered lowly
'How dark the woods will be!

'The thick leaves in my murmur
'Are rustling like a dream,
'And all their myriad voices
'Instinct with spirit seem.'

I said: 'Go gentle singer,
'Thy wooing voice is kind
'But do not think its music
'Has power to reach my mind.

'Play with the scented flower,
'The young tree's supple bough –
'And leave my human feelings
'In their own course to flow.'

The wanderer would not leave me
Its kiss grew warmer still –
'O come', it sighed so sweetly,
'I'll win thee 'gainst thy will.

'Have we not been from childhood friends?
'Have I not loved thee long?
'As long as thou hast loved the night
'Whose silence wakes my song.

'And when thy heart is laid at rest
'Beneath the church–yard stone
'I shall have time enough to mourn
'And thou to be alone.'

11 September 1840

THERE LET THY BLEEDING
BRANCH ATONE

There let thy bleeding branch atone
For every torturing tear:
Shall my young sins, my sins alone,
Be everlasting here?

Who bade thee keep that cursed name
A pledge for memory?
As if Oblivion ever came
To breathe its bliss on me;

As if, through all the 'wildering maze
Of mad hours left behind,
I once forgot the early days
That thou wouldst call to mind.

AND LIKE MYSELF LONE,
WHOLLY LONE

And like myself lone, wholly lone,
It sees the day's long sunshine glow;
And like myself it makes its moan
In unexhausted woe.

Give we the hills our equal prayer:
Earth's breezy hills and heaven's blue sea;
We ask for nothing further here
But our own hearts and liberty.

Ah! could my hand unlock its chain,
How gladly would I watch it soar,
And ne'er regret and ne'er complain
To see its shining eyes no more.

But let me think that if today
It pines in cold captivity,
Tomorrow both shall soar away
Eternally, entirely free.

27 February 1841

RICHES I HOLD IN LIGHT ESTEEM

Riches I hold in light esteem
And Love I laugh to scorn
And Lust of Fame was but a dream
That vanished with the morn –

And if I pray – the only prayer
That moves my lips for me
Is – 'Leave the heart that now I bear
And give me liberty'.

Yes, as my swift days near their goal
'Tis all that I implore –
Through life and death, a chainless soul
With courage to endure!

1 March 1841

THIS HEART SHOULD REST

Methinks this heart should rest awhile,
So stilly round the evening falls;
The veiled sun sheds no parting smile,
Nor mirth, nor music wakes my halls.

I have sat lonely all the day
Watching the drizzly mist descend
And first conceal the hills in grey
And then along the valleys wend.

And I have sat and watched the trees
And the sad flowers – how drear they blow:
Those flowers were formed to feel the breeze
Wave their light leaves in summer's glow.

Yet their lives passed in gloomy woe
And hopeless comes its dark decline,
And I lament, because I know
That cold departure pictures mine.

SHALL EARTH NO MORE INSPIRE THEE?

Shall Earth no more inspire thee,
Thou lonely dreamer now?
Since passion may not fire thee
Shall Nature cease to bow?

Thy mind is ever moving
In regions dark to thee;
Recall its useless roving –
Come back and dwell with me.

I know my mountain-breezes
Enchant and soothe thee still –
I know my sunshine pleases
Despite thy wayward will.

When day with evening blending
Sinks from the summer sky,
I've seen thy spirit bending
In fond idolatry.

I've watched thee every hour –
I know my mighty sway –
I know my magic power
To drive thy griefs away.

Few hearts to mortals given
On earth so wildly pine
Yet none would ask a Heaven
More like the Earth than thine.

Then let my winds caress thee –
Thy comrade let me be –
Since nought beside can bless thee
Return and dwell with me.

16 May 1841

Aye, there it is! It wakes tonight
Sweet thoughts that will not die
And feeling's fires flash all as bright
As in the years gone by!

And I can tell by thine altered cheek
And by thy kindled gaze
And by the word thou scarce dost speak,
How wildly fancy plays.

Yes I could swear that glorious wind
Has swept the world aside
Has dashed its memory from thy mind
Like foam-bells from the tide –

And thou art now a spirit pouring
Thy presence into all –
The essence of the Tempest's roaring
And of the Tempest's fall –

A universal influence
From Thine own influence free –
A principle of life intense
Lost to mortality.

Thus truly when that breast is cold
Thy prisoned soul shall rise,
The dungeon mingle with the mould –
The captive with the skies.

6 July 1841

y
/ay.
tread
ad;
.e mould
—
the tears
m vanished years;
d Mortal pain
not heal again.

Let me ~~~~~~~~ f the woe
I've seen and hear~ nd felt below,
And Heaven itself, so pure and blest,
Could never give my spirit rest.
Sweet land of light! thy children fair
Know nought akin to our despair;
Nor have they felt, nor can they tell
What tenants haunt each mortal cell,
What gloomy guests we hold within —
Torments and madness, tears and sin!
Well, may they live in ecstasy
Their long eternity of joy;
At least we would not bring them down
With us to weep, with us to groan.
No — Earth would wish no other sphere
To taste her cup of sufferings drear;
She turns from Heaven a careless eye
And only mourns that *we* must die!
Ah mother, what shall comfort thee
In all this endless misery?
To cheer our eager eyes a while
We see thee smile; how fondly smile!
But who reads not through that tender glow

Thy deep, unutterable woe?
Indeed no dazzling land above
Can cheat thee of thy children's love.
We all in life's departing shine
Our last dear longings blend with thine;
And struggle still, and strive to trace
With clouded gaze thy darling face.
We would not leave our native home
For *any* world beyond the Tomb.
No – rather on thy kindly breast
Let us be laid in lasting rest
Or waken but to share with thee
A mutual immortality.

17 July 1841

THE EVENING PASSES FAST AWAY

The evening passes fast away,
'Tis almost time to rest;
What thoughts has left the vanished day?
What feelings in thy breast?

'The vanished day? It leaves a sense
'Of labour hardly done –
'Of little gained with vast expense –
'A sense of grief alone!

'Time stands before the door of Death
'Upbraiding bitterly
'And Conscience with exhaustless breath
'Pours black reproach on me:

'And though I think that Conscience lies
'And Time should Fate condemn,
'Still weak Repentance clouds my eyes
'And makes me yield to them!'

Then art thou glad to seek repose?
Art glad to leave the sea?
And anchor all thy weary woes
In calm Eternity?

Nothing regrets to see thee go –
Not one voice sobs, 'Farewell'
And where thy heart has suffered so
Canst thou desire to dwell?

'Alas! the countless links are strong
'That bind us to our clay;
'The loving spirit lingers long
'And would not pass away –

'And rest is sweet, when laurelled fame
'Will crown the soldier's crest;
'But a brave heart with a tarnished name
'Would rather fight, than rest.'

Well thou hast fought for many a year,
Hast fought thy whole life through,
Hast humbled Falsehood, trampled Fear;
What is there left to do?

' 'Tis true – this arm has hotly striven,
'Has dared what few would dare;
'Much have I done, and freely given,
'Yet little learnt to bear!'

Look on the grave where thou must sleep,
Thy last and strongest foe –
'Twill be endurance not to weep
If that repose be woe.

The long fight closing in defeat –
Defeat serenely borne –
Thine eventide may still be sweet,
Thy night a glorious morn.

23 October 1842 – 6 February 1843

HOW CLEAR SHE SHINES!

How clear she shines! How quietly
I lie beneath her silver light
While Heaven and Earth are whispering me,
'Tomorrow wake – but dream tonight'.

Yes – Fancy come, my fairy love!
These throbbing temples, softly kiss,
And bend my lonely couch above
And bring me rest, and bring me bliss.

The world is going. Dark world adieu!
Grim world, go hide thee till the day:
The heart thou canst not all subdue
Must still resist if thou delay.

Thy love I will not –will not share
Thy hatred only wakes a smile
Thy griefs may wound – thy wrongs may tear
But O, thy lies shall not beguile.

While gazing on the stars that glow
Above me in that stormless sea
I long to hope that all the woe
Creation knows is held in thee!

And this shall be my dream tonight –
I'll think the heaven of glorious spheres
Is rolling on its course of light
In endless bliss, through endless years.

I'll think, there's not one world above,
Far as these straining eyes can see,
Where Wisdom ever laughed at Love –
Or Virtue crouched to Infamy.

Where writhing 'neath the strokes of Fate
The mangled wretch was forced to smile
To match his patience 'gainst her hate,
His heart rebellious all the while.

Where Pleasure still will lead to wrong
And helpless Reason warn in vain
And Truth is weak, and Treachery strong
And Joy the shortest path to pain:

And peace this lethargy of grief,
And Hope a phantom of the soul –
And Life a labour void and brief –
And Death the despot of the whole.

13 April 1843

WHERE BEAMS THE SUN

Where beams the sun the brightest
In the noons of sweet July?
Where falls the snow the lightest
From bleak December's sky?

Where can the weary lay his head
And lay it safe the while
In a grave that never shuts its dead
From heaven's benignant smile?

Upon the earth in sunlight
Spring grass grows green and fair
But beneath the earth is midnight –
Eternal midnight there!

Then why lament that those we love
Escape Earth's dungeon tomb?
As if the flowers that blow above
Could charm its undergloom.

From morning's faintest dawning
Till evening's deepest shade
Thou wilt not cease thy mourning
To know where she is laid.

But if to weep above her grave
Be such a priceless boon
Go, shed thy tears in Ocean's wave
And they will reach it soon.

Yet midst thy wild repining
Mad though that anguish be
Think heaven on her is shining
Even as it shines on thee.

With thy mind's vision pierce the Deep
Look how she rests below
And tell me, why such blessèd sleep
Should cause such bitter woe?

1 May 1843

IN THE EARTH, THE EARTH THOU SHALT BE LAID

In the earth, the earth thou shalt be laid
A grey stone standing over thee;
Black mould beneath thee spread
And black mould to cover thee.

'Well, there is rest there
'So fast come thy prophecy –
'The time when my sunny hair
'Shall with grass roots twinéd be.'

But cold, cold is that resting place
Shut out from Joy and Liberty
And all who loved thy living face
Will shrink from its gloom and thee.

'No so, *here* the world is chill
'And sworn friends fall from me
'But *there*, they'll own me still
'And prize my memory.'

Farewell then, all that love
All that deep sympathy:
Sleep on, heaven laughs above,
Earth never misses thee.

Turf-sod and tombstone drear
Part human company;
One heart broke, only, there
That heart was worthy thee!

6 September 1843

HOPE

Hope was but a timid Friend –
She sat without my grated den
Watching how my fate would tend
Even as selfish-hearted men.

She was cruel in her fear.
Through the bars, one dreary day,
I looked out to see her there
And she turned her face away!

Like a false guard false watch keeping
Still in strife she whispered peace;
She would sing while I was weeping,
If I listened, she would cease.

False she was, and unrelenting.
When my last joys strewed the ground
Even Sorrow saw repenting
Those sad relics scattered round;

Hope – whose whisper would have given
Balm to all that frenzied pain –
Stretched her wings and soared to heaven;
Went – and ne'er returned again!

18 December 1843 (or 1844)

EMILY BRONTË

AT CASTLE WOOD

The day is done, the winter sun
Is setting in its sullen sky;
And drear the course that has been run,
And dim the beams that slowly die.

No star will light my coming night;
No moon of hope for me will shine;
I mourn not heaven would blast my sight,
And I never longed for ways divine.

Through Life's hard Task I did not ask
Celestial aid, celestial cheer:
I saw my fate without its mask,
And met it too without a tear.

The grief that prest this living breast
Was heavier far than earth can be;
And who would dread eternal rest
When labour's hire was agony?

Dark falls the fear of this despair
On spirits born for happiness;
But I was bred the mate of care,
The foster-child of sore distress.

No sighs for me, no sympathy,
No wish to keep my soul below;
The heart is dead since infancy,
Unwept-for let the body go.

2 February 1844

MY COMFORTER

Well hast thou spoken – and yet not taught
A feeling strange or new;
Thou hast but raised a latent thought,
A cloud-closed beam of sunshine brought
To gleam in open view.

Deep down – concealed within my soul
That light lies hid from men,
Yet glows unquenched – though shadows roll,
Its gentle ray cannot control,
About the sullen den.

Was I not vexed, in these gloomy ways
To walk unlit so long?
Around me, wretches uttering praise
Or howling o'er their hopeless days,
And each with Frenzy's tongue –

A Brotherhood of misery,
With smiles as sad as sighs;
Their madness daily maddening me,
And turning into agony
The Bliss before my eyes.

So stood I, in Heaven's glorious sun
And in the glare of Hell
My spirit drank a mingled tone
Of seraph's song and demon's groan –
What thy soul bore thy soul alone
Within its self may tell.

Like a soft air above a sea
Tossed by the tempest's stir –
A thaw-wind melting quietly
The snowdrift on some wintery lea
No – what sweet thing can match with thee,
My thoughtful Comforter?

And yet a little longer speak
Calm this resentful mood
And while the savage heart grows meek,
For other token do not seek,
But let the tear upon my cheek
Evince my gratitude.

10 February 1844

COME, WALK WITH ME

Come, walk with me,
There's only thee
To bless my spirit now –
We used to love on winter nights
To wander through the snow;
Can we not woo back old delights?
The clouds rush dark and wild,
They fleck with shade our mountain heights
The same as long ago
And on the horizon rest at last
In looming masses piled;
While moonbeams flash and fly so fast
We scarce can say they smiled.

Come walk with me – come, walk with me;
We were not once so few,
But Death has stolen our company
As sunshine steals the dew.
He took them one by one and we
Are left the only two;
So closer would my feelings twine
Because they have no stay but thine.

'Nay, call me not; it may not be –
Is human love so true?
Can Friendship's flower droop on for years
And then revive anew?
No, though the soil be wet with tears
How fair so'er it grew
The vital sap once perishéd
Will never flow again
And surer than that dwelling dread,
The narrow dungeon of the Dead,
Time parts the hearts of men.'

THE LINNET IN THE ROCKY DELLS

The linnet in the rocky dells,
The moor-lark in the air,
The bee among the heather-bells
That hide my lady fair —

The wild deer browse above her breast;
The wild birds raise their brood,
And they, her smiles of love carest,
Have left her solitude!

I ween, that when the grave's dark wall
Did first her form retain
They thought their hearts could ne'er recall
The light of joy again.

They thought the tide of grief would flow
Unchecked through future years
But where is all their anguish now,
And where are all their tears?

Well, let them fight for Honour's breath,
Or Pleasure's shade pursue —
The Dweller in the land of Death
Is changed and careless too.

And if their eyes should watch and weep
Till sorrow's source were dry
She would not in her tranquil sleep
Return a single sigh.

Blow, west-wind, by the lonely mound
And murmur, summer streams;
There is no need of other sound
To soothe my Lady's dreams.
1 May 1844

TO IMAGINATION

When weary with the long day's care
And earthly change from pain to pain
And lost and ready to despair
Thy kind voice calls me back again.
O my true friend, I am not lone
While thou canst speak with such a tone!

So hopeless is the world without
The world within I doubly prize –
Thy world where guile and hate and doubt
And cold suspicion never rise –
Where thou and I and Liberty
Hold undisputed sovereignty.

What matter it that all around
Danger and guilt and darkness lie
If but within our bosom's bound
We hold a bright unsullied sky
Warm with the thousand mingled rays
Of suns that know no winter days?

Reason indeed may oft complain
For Nature's sad reality
And tell the suffering heart how vain
Its cherished dreams must always be
And Truth may rudely trample down
The flowers of Fancy newly blown.

But thou art ever there to bring
The hovering visions back and breathe
New glories o'er the blighted spring
And call a lovelier life from death
And whisper with a voice divine
Of real worlds as bright as thine.

I trust not to thy phantom bliss
Yet still in evening's quiet hour
With never-failing thankfulness
I welcome thee, benignant power,
Sure solacer of human cares
And brighter hope when hope despairs.

3 September 1844

O THY BRIGHT EYES
MUST ANSWER NOW

O thy bright eyes must answer now,
When Reason, with a scornful brow,
Is mocking at my overthrow;
O thy sweet tongue must plead for me
And tell why I have chosen thee!

Stern Reason is to judgement come
Arrayed in all her forms of gloom:
Wilt thou my advocate be dumb?
No, radiant angel, speak and say
Why I did cast the world away;

Why I have persevered to shun
The common paths that others run
And on a strange road journeyed on;
Heedless alike of Wealth and Power –
Of Glory's wreath and Pleasure's flower.

These once indeed seemed Beings divine
And they perchance heard vows of mine
And saw my offerings on their shrine –
But, careless gifts are seldom prized
And mine were worthily despised;

So with a ready heart I swore
To seek their altar-stone no more
And gave my spirit to adore
Thee, ever present, phantom thing –
My slave, my comrade, and my king!

A slave because I rule thee still
Incline thee to my changeful will
And make thy influence good or ill –
A comrade, for by day and night
Thou art my intimate Delight –

My Darling Pain that wounds and sears
And wrings a blessing out from tears
By deadening me to real cares:
And yet a king – though Prudence well
Have taught thy subject to rebel.

And am I wrong, to worship where
Faith cannot doubt, nor Hope despair,
Since my own soul can grant my prayer?
Speak God of Visions, plead for me,
And tell why I have chosen thee!

14 October 1844

THE PHILOSOPHER'S CONCLUSION

'Enough of Thought, Philosopher;
Too long hast thou been dreaming
Unlightened, in this chamber drear
While summer's sun is beaming –
Space-sweeping soul, what sad refrain
Concludes thy musings once again?

'O for the time when I shall sleep
'Without identity –
'And never care how rain may steep
'Or snow may cover me!

'No promised Heaven, these wild Desires
'Could all or half fulfil –
'No threatened Hell, with quenchless fires,
'Subdue this quenchless will!'

– So said I, and still say the same;
– Still to my death will say –
Three Gods within this little frame
Are warring night and day.

Heaven could not hold them all, and yet
They all are held in me
And must be mine till I forget
My present entity.

O for the time when in my breast
Their struggles will be o'er;
O for the day when I shall rest
And never suffer more!

'I saw a spirit standing, Man,
'Where thou dost stand – an hour ago;
'And round his feet three rivers ran
'Of equal depth and equal flow –

'A Golden Stream, and one like blood
'And one like sapphire, seemed to be
'But where they joined their triple flood
'It tumbled in an inky sea.

'The spirit bent his dazzling gaze
'Down on that Ocean's gloomy night,
'Then – kindling all with sudden blaze,
'The glad deep sparkled wide and bright –
'White as the sun, far more fair
'Than their divided sources were!'

– And even for that spirit, Seer,
I've watched and sought my lifetime long;
Sought him in Heaven, Hell, Earth and Air
An endless search – and always wrong!

Had I but seen his glorious eye
Once light the clouds that 'wilder me,
I ne'er had raised this coward cry
To cease to think and cease to be –

I ne'er had called oblivion blest
Nor stretching eager hands to Death
Implored to change for lifeless rest
This sentient soul, this living breath.

O let me die, that power and will
Their cruel strife may close,
And vanquished Good, victorious Ill
Be lost in one repose.

3 February 1845

COLD IN THE EARTH

Cold in the earth and the deep snow piled above
    thee!
Far, far removed, cold in the dreary grave!
Have I forgot, my Only Love, to love thee,
Severed at last by Time's all-wearing wave?

Now, when alone, do my thoughts no longer hover
Over the mountains on Angora's shore;
Resting their wings where heath and fern-leaves
    cover
That noble heart for ever, ever more?

Cold in the earth, and fifteen wild Decembers
From those brown hills have melted into spring –
Faithful indeed is the spirit that remembers
After such years of change and suffering!

Sweet Love of youth, forgive if I forget thee
While the World's tide is bearing me along:
Sterner desires and darker hopes beset me,
Hopes which obscure but cannot do thee wrong.

No other Sun has lightened up my heaven;
No other Star has ever shone for me:
All my life's bliss from thy dear life was given –
All my life's bliss is in the grave with thee.

But when the days of golden dreams had perished
And even Despair was powerless to destroy,
Then did I learn how existence could be cherished,
Strengthened and fed without the aid of joy.

Then did I check the tears of useless passion,
Weaned my young soul from yearning after thine;
Sternly denied its burning wish to hasten
Down to that tomb already more than mine!

And even yet, I dare not let it languish,
Dare not indulge in Memory's rapturous pain:
Once drinking deep of that divinest anguish,
How could I seek the empty world again?

3 March 1845

DEATH

Death, that struck when I was most confiding
In my certain Faith of Joy to be,
Strike again, Time's withered branch dividing
From the fresh root of Eternity!

Leaves, upon Time's branch, were growing
   brightly
Full of sap and full of silver dew;
Birds, beneath its shelter, gathered nightly;
Daily, round its flowers, the wild birds flew.

Sorrow passed and plucked the golden blossom,
Guilt stripped off the foliage in its pride;
But within its parent's kindly bosom
Flowed forever Life's restoring tide.

Little mourned I for the parted Gladness,
For the vacant nest and silent song;
Hope was there and laughed me out of sadness,
Whispering, 'Winter will not linger long'.

And behold, with tenfold increase blessing
Spring adorned the beauty-burdened spray;
Wind and rain and fervent heat caressing
Lavished glory on its second May.

High it rose; no wingéd grief could sweep it;
Sin was scared to distance with its shine:
Love and its own life had power to keep it
From all wrong, from every blight but thine!

Heartless Death, the young leaves droop and languish!
Evening's gentle air may still restore –
No, the morning sunshine mocks my anguish –
Time for me must never blossom more!

Strike it down – that other boughs may flourish
Where that perished sapling used to be;
Thus, at least, its mouldering corpse will nourish
That from which it sprung – Eternity.

10 April 1845

STARS

Ah! why, because the dazzling sun
Restored my earth to joy
Have you departed, every one,
And left a desert sky?

All through the night, your glorious eyes
Were gazing down in mine
And with a full heart's thankful sighs
I blessed that watch divine!

I was at peace – and drank your beams
As they were life to me
And revelled in my changeful dreams
Like petrel on the sea.

Thought followed thought – star followed star
Through boundless regions on
While one sweet influence, near and far,
Thrilled through and proved us one.

Why did the morning rise to break
So great, so pure a spell,
And scorch with fire the tranquil cheek
Where your cool radiance fell?

Blood red he rose, and arrow-straight
His fierce beams struck my brow:
The soul of Nature sprang elate,
But mine sank sad and low!

My lids closed down – yet through their veil
I saw him blazing still;
And bathe in gold the misty dale
And flash upon the hill.

I turned me to the pillow then
To call back Night, and see
Your worlds of solemn light, again
Throb with my heart and me!

It would not do – the pillow glowed
And glowed both roof and floor
And birds sang loudly in the wood,
And fresh winds shook the door.

The curtains waved, the wakened flies
Were murmuring round my room
Imprisoned there, till I should rise
And give them leave to roam.

O stars and dreams and Gentle Night –
O Night and stars return!
And hide me from the hostile light
That does not warm, but burn –

That drains the blood of suffering men –
Drinks tears, instead of dew –
Let me sleep through his blinding reign
And only wake with you!

14 April 1845

HEAVY HANGS THE RAINDROP

Heavy hangs the raindrop
From the burdened spray;
Heavy broods the damp mist
On Uplands far away;

Heavy looms the dull sky,
Heavy rolls the sea –
And heavy beats the young heart
Beneath that lonely tree.

Never has a blue streak
Cleft the clouds since morn –
Never has his grim Fate
Smiled since he was born.

Frowning on the infant,
Shadowing childhood's joy;
Guardian angel knows not
That melancholy boy.

Day is passing swiftly
Its sad and sombre prime;
Youth is fast invading
Sterner manhood's time.

All the flowers are praying
For sun before they close
And he prays too, unknowing,
That sunless human rose!

Blossoms, that the west wind
Has never wooed to blow
Scentless are your petals,
Your dew as cold as snow.

Soul, where kindred kindness
No early promise woke
Barren is your beauty
As weed upon the rock.

Wither, Brothers, wither,
You were vainly given –
Earth reserves no blessing
For the unblest of Heaven!

28 May 1845

CHILD OF DELIGHT

Child of delight! with sun-bright hair
And seablue seadeep eyes;
Spirit of Bliss, what brings thee here
Beneath these sullen skies?

Thou shouldest live in eternal spring
Where endless day is never dim;
Why, seraph, has thy erring wing
Borne thee down to weep with him?

'Ah! not from heaven am I descended
'And I do not come to mingle tears
'But sweet is day though with shadows blended
'And, though clouded, sweet are youthful years.

'I, the image of light and gladness,
'Saw and pitied that mournful boy
'And I swore to take his gloomy sadness
'And give to him my beamy joy.

'Heavy and dark the night is closing
'Heavy and dark may its biding be
'Better for all from grief reposing
'And better for all who watch like me.

'Guardian angel he lacks no longer;
'Evil fortune he need not fear:
'Fate is strong, but Love is stronger
'And more unsleeping than angel's care.'

May 1845

HOW BEAUTIFUL THE EARTH IS STILL

How beautiful the Earth is still
To thee, how full of Happiness;
How little fraught with real ill
Or shadowy phantoms of distress;

How Spring can bring thee glory yet,
And Summer win thee to forget
December's sullen time!
Why dost thou hold the treasure fast
Of youth's delight, when youth is past
And thou art near thy prime?

When those who were thy own compeers
Equal in fortunes and in years
Have seen their morning melt in tears
To dull unlovely day;
Blest, had they died unproved and young
Before their hearts were wildly wrung
Poor slaves, subdued by passions strong
A weak and helpless prey!

'Because, I hoped while they enjoyed
'And by fulfilment, hope destroyed —
'As children hope, with trustful breast
'I waited Bliss and cherished Rest.

'A thoughtful Spirit taught me soon
'That we must long till life be done
'That every phase of earthly joy
'Will always fade and always cloy —

'This I foresaw, and would not chase
'The fleeting treacheries
'But with firm foot and tranquil face
'Held backward from that tempting race;
'Gazed o'er the sands the waves efface
'To the enduring seas –

'There cast my anchor of Desire
'Deep in unknown Eternity,
'Nor ever let my Spirit tire
'With looking for *What is to be*.

'It is Hope's spell that glorifies
'Like youth to my maturer eyes
'All Nature's million mysteries –
'The fearful and the fair –

'Hope soothes me in the griefs I know
'She lulls my pain for other's woe
'And makes me strong to undergo
'What I am born to bear.

'Glad comforter, will I not brave
'Unawed, the darkness of the grave?
'Nay, smile to hear Death's billows rave,
'My guide, sustained by thee?
'The more unjust seems present fate
'The more my spirit springs elate
'Strong in thy strength, to anticipate
'Rewarding Destiny!'

2 June 1845

SILENT IS THE HOUSE

Silent is the House – all are laid asleep;
One, alone, looks out o'er the snowwreaths deep;
Watching every cloud, dreading every breeze
That whirls the 'wildering drifts and bends the
    groaning trees.

Cheerful is the hearth, soft the matted floor;
Not one shivering gust creeps through pane or door;
The little lamp burns straight, its rays shoot strong
    and far:
I trim it well to be the Wanderer's guiding-star.

Frown my haughty sire; chide my angry dame,
Set your slaves to spy, threaten me with shame:
But neither sire nor dame, nor prying serf shall know
What angel nightly tracks that waste of winter snow.

In the dungeon crypts idly did I stray,
Reckless of the lives wasting there away:
'Draw the ponderous bars; open Warder stern!'
He dare not say me nay – the hinges harshly turn.

'Our guests are darkly lodged,' I whispered gazing
    through
The vault whose grated eye showed heaven more
    grey than blue.
(This was when the glad spring laughed in awaking
    pride):
'Aye, darkly lodged enough!' returned my sullen
    guide.

Then, God forgive my youth, forgive my careless
    tongue!
I scoffed as the chill chains on the damp flagstones
    rung;
'Confined in triple walls, art thou so much to fear,
'That we must bind thee down and clench thy fetters
    here?'

The captive raised her face; it was as soft and mild
As sculptured marble saint or slumbering, unweaned
    child;
It was so soft and mild, it was so sweet and fair
Pain could not trace a line nor grief a shadow there!

The captive raised her hand and pressed it to her
    brow:
'I have been struck,' she said, 'and I am suffering
    now;
'Yet these are little worth, your bolts and irons strong
'And were they forged in steel they could not hold me
    long'.

Hoarse laughed the jailor grim: 'Shall I be won to
    hear
'Dost think, fond dreaming wretch, that *I* shall grant
    thy prayer?
'Or better still, wilt melt my master's heart with
    groans?
'Ah sooner might the sun thaw down these granite
    stones!

'My master's voice is low, his aspect bland and kind
'But hard as hardest flint the soul that lurks behind;
'And I am rough and rude, yet not more rough to see
'Than is the hidden ghost which has its home in me.'

About her lips there played a smile of almost scorn:
'My friend,' she gently said, 'you have not heard me
    mourn;
'When you my parents' lives – *my* lost life can restore
'Then may I weep and sue, but *never*, friend, before!'

Her head sank on her hands; its fair curls swept the
    ground;
The dungeon seemed to swim in strange confusion
    round –
'Is she so near to death?' I murmured half aloud
And kneeling, parted back the floating golden cloud.

Alas, how former days upon my heart were borne;
How memory mirrored then the prisoner's joyous
    morn;
Too blithe, too loving child, too warmly, wildly gay!
Was that the wintry close of thy celestial May?

She knew me and she sighed, 'Lord Julian, can it be,
'Of all my playmates, you, alone, remember me?
'Nay start not at my words, unless you deem it shame
'To own, from conquered foe, a once familiar name.

'I cannot wonder now at ought the world will do,
'And insult and contempt I lightly brook from you,
'Since those who vowed away their souls to win my
    love
'Around this living grave like utter strangers move!

'Nor has one voice been raised to plead that I might die,
'Nor buried under earth but in the open sky;
'By ball or speedy knife or headsman's skilful blow –
'A quick and welcome pang instead of lingering woe!

'Yet, tell them, Julian, all, I am not doomed to wear
'Year after year in gloom and desolate despair;
'A messenger of Hope comes every night to me
'And offers, for short life, eternal liberty.

'He comes with western winds, with evening's
       wandering airs,
'With that clear dusk of heaven that brings the thickest
       stars;
'Winds take a pensive tone and stars a tender fire
'And visions rise and change which kill me with desire –

'Desire for nothing known in my maturer years
'When joy grew mad with awe at counting future
       tears;
'When, if my spirit's sky was full of flashes warm,
'I knew not whence they came, from sun or thunderstorm;

'But first a hush of peace, a soundless calm descends;
'The struggle of distress and fierce impatience ends;
'Mute music soothes my breast – unuttered harmony
'That I could never dream till earth was lost to me.

'Then dawns the Invisible, the Unseen its truth
       reveals;
'My outward sense is gone, my inward essence feels –
'Its wings are almost free, its home, its harbour found;
'Measuring the gulf it stoops and dares the final
       bound!

'Oh dreadful is the check – intense the agony
'When the ear begins to hear and the eye begins to see;
'When the pulse begins to throb, the brain to think
   again;
'The soul to feel the flesh and the flesh to feel the
   chain!

'Yet I would lose no sting, would wish no torture less;
'The more that anguish racks the earlier it will bless;
'And robed in fires of Hell, or bright with heavenly
   shine
'If it but herald Death, the vision is divine!'

She ceased to speak and I, unanswering watched her
   there,
Not daring now to touch one lock of silken hair –
As I had knelt in scorn, on the dank floor I knelt still,
My fingers in the links of that iron hard and chill.

I heard, and yet heard not, the surly keeper growl;
I saw, yet did not see, the flagstone damp and foul.
The keeper, to and fro, paced by the bolted door
And shivered as he walked and as he shivered, swore.

While my cheek glowed in flame, I marked that he
   did rave
Of air that froze his blood and moisture like the
   grave –
'We have been two hours good!' he muttered peevishly;
Then, loosing off his belt the rusty key,

He said, 'You may be pleased, Lord Julian, still to stay
'But duty will not let me linger here all day;
'If I might go, I'd leave this badge of mine with you,
'Not doubting that you'd prove a jailor stern and true'.

I took the proffered charge; the captive's drooping lid
Beneath its shady lash a sudden lightning hid:
Earth's hope was not so dead, heaven's home was not
    so dear;
I read it in that flash of of longing quelled by fear.

Then like a tender child whose hand did just enfold
Safe in its eager grasp a bird it wept to hold,
When pierced with one wild glance from the troubled
    hazel eye,
It gushes into tears and lets its treasure fly –

Thus ruth and selfish love together striving tore
The heart all newly taught to pity and adore;
If I should break the chain I felt my bird would go;
Yet I must break the chain or seal the prisoner's woe.

Short strife: what rest could soothe – what peace could
    visit me
While she lay pining there for Death to set her free?
'Rochelle, the dungeons teem with foes to gorge our
    hate –
'Thou art too young to die by such a bitter fate!'

With hurried blow on blow I struck the fetters through
Regardless how that deed my after hours might rue.
Oh, I was over-blest by the warm unasked embrace –
By the smile of grateful joy that lit her angel face!

And I was over-blest – aye, more than I could dream
When, faint, she turned aside from noon's unwonted
    beam;
When though the cage was wide – the heaven around
    it lay –
Its pinion would not waft my wounded dove away.

Through thirteen anxious weeks of terror-blent
    delight
I guarded her by day and guarded her by night
While foes were prowling near and Death gazed
    greedily
And only Hope remained a faithful friend to me.

Then oft with taunting smile, I heard my kindred tell
'How Julian loved his hearth and sheltering roof-tree
    well;
'How the trumpet's voice might call, the battle-
    standard wave,
'But Julian had no heart to fill a patriot's grave.'

And I, who am so quick to answer sneer with sneer
So ready to condemn, to scorn a coward's fear,
I held my peace like one whose conscience keeps him
    dumb
And saw my kinsmen go – and lingered still at home.

Another hand than mine my rightful banner held
And gathered my renown on Freedom's crimson field;
Yet I had no desire the glorious prize to gain –
It needed braver nerve to face the world's disdain.

And by the patient strength that could that world
    defy,
By suffering with calm mind, contempt and calumny;
By never-doubting love, unswerving constancy,
Rochelle, I earned at last an equal love from thee!

9 October 1845

NO COWARD SOUL IS MINE

No coward soul is mine
No trembler in the world's storm-troubled sphere
I see Heaven's glories shine
And Faith shines equal arming me from Fear.

O God within my breast
Almighty ever-present Deity
Life, that in me hast rest
As I, Undying Life, have power in thee.

Vain are the thousand creeds
That move men's hearts, unutterably vain,
Worthless as withered weeds
Or idlest froth amid the boundless main

To waken doubt in one
Holding so fast by thy infinity
So surely anchored on
The steadfast rock of Immortality.

With wide-embracing love
Thy spirit animates eternal years
Pervades and broods above,
Changes, sustains, dissolves, creates and rears.

Though earth and moon were gone,
And suns and universes ceased to be
And thou wert left alone
Every Existence would exist in thee.

There is not room for Death
Nor atom that his might could render void
Since thou art Being and Breath
And what thou art may never be destroyed.

2 January 1846

WHY ASK TO KNOW THE DATE – THE CLIME?

Why ask to know the date – the clime?
More than mere words they cannot be:
Men knelt to God and worshipped crime,
And crushed the helpless, even as we.

But they had learnt from length of strife –
Of civil war and anarchy
To laugh at death and look on life
With somewhat lighter sympathy.

It was the autumn of the year;
The time to labouring peasants dear:
Week after week, from noon to noon,
September shone as bright as June.
Still, never hand a sickle held;
The crops were garnered in the field –
Trod out, and ground by horses' feet
While every ear was milky sweet;
And kneaded on the threshing floor
With mire of tears and human gore.
Some said, they thought that heaven's pure rain
Would hardly bless those fields again:
Not so – the all-benignant skies
Rebuked that fear of famished eyes –
July passed on with showers and dew,
And August glowed in showerless blue;
No harvest time could be more fair
Had harvest fruits but ripened there.

And I confess that hate of rest,
And thirst for things abandoned now,
Had weaned me from my country's breast
And brought me to that land of woe.

Enthusiast – in a name delighting;
My alien sword I drew to free
One race, beneath two standards fighting,
For loyalty and liberty.

When kindred strive – God help the weak!
A brother's ruth 'tis vain to seek:
At first, it hurt my chivalry
To join them in their cruelty;
But I grew hard – I learnt to wear
An iron front to terror's prayer;
I learnt to turn my ears away
From torture's groans, as well as they.

By force I learnt – what power had I
To say the conquered should not die?
What heart, one trembling foe to save
When hundreds daily filled the grave?
Yet, there *were* faces that could move
A moment's flash of human love;
And there were fates that made me feel
I was not to the centre, steel.

I've often witnessed wise men fear
To meet distress which they foresaw;
And seeming cowards nobly bear
A doom that thrilled the brave with awe:

Strange proofs I've seen, how hearts could hide
Their secret with a life-long pride.
And then, reveal it as they died –
Strange courage, and strange weakness too,
In that last hour when most are true,
And timid natures strangely nerved
To deeds from which the desperate swerved.

These I may tell, but leave them now.
Go with me where my thoughts would go;
Now all today, and all last night
I've had one scene before my sight –

Wood-shadowed dales; a harvest moon
Unclouded in its glorious noon;
A solemn landscape, wide and still;
A red fire on a distant hill –
A line of fires, and deep below,
Another dusker, drearier glow –
Charred beams, and lime, and blackened stones
Self-piled in cairns o'er burning bones
And lurid flames that licked the wood
Then quenched their glare in pools of blood.

But yestereve – No! never care;
Let street and suburb smoulder there –
Smoke hidden, in the winding glen,
They lay too far to vex my ken.
Four score shot down – all veterans strong –
One prisoner spared, their leader young –
And he within his house was laid,
Wounded, and weak and nearly dead.
We gave him life against his will;
For he entreated us to kill –
But statue-like we saw his tears –
And coldly fell our captain's sneers!

'Now heaven forbid!' with scorn he said,
'That noble gore our hands should shed
'Like common blood – retain thy breath
'Or scheme if thou canst purchase death.
'When men are poor we sometimes hear
'And pitying grant that dastard prayer;

'When men are rich, we make them buy
'The pleasant privilege, to die.
'O, we have castles reared for kings,
'Embattled towers and buttressed wings,
'Thrice three feet thick, and guarded well
'With chain, and bolt, and sentinel!
'We build our despots' dwellings sure,
'Knowing they love to live secure.
'And our respect for royalty
'Extends to thy estate and thee!'

The suppliant groaned, his moistened eye
Swam wild and dim with agony.
The gentle blood could ill sustain
Degrading taunts, unhonoured pain.
Bold had he shown himself to lead;
Eager to smite and proud to bleed –
A man, amid the battle's storm:
An infant in the after calm.

Beyond the town his mansions stood
Girt round with pasture-land and wood;
And there our wounded soldiers lying
Enjoyed the ease of wealth in dying.
For him, no mortal more than he
Had softened life with luxury;
And truly did our priest declare
'Of good things he had had his share.'

We lodged him in an empty place,
The full moon beaming on his face,
Through shivered glass, and ruins, made
Where shell and ball the fiercest played.

I watched his ghastly couch beside
Regardless if he lived or died –
Nay, muttering curses on the breast
Whose ceaseless moans denied me rest.

'Twas hard, I know, 'twas harsh to say,
'Hell snatch thy worthless soul away!'
But then 'twas hard my lids to keep,
Through the long night, estranged from sleep.
Captive and keeper, both outworn,
Each in his misery yearned for morn;
Even though returning morn should bring
Intenser toil and suffering.

Slow, slow it came! Our dreary room
Grew drearier with departing gloom;
Yet, as the west wind warmly blew
I felt my pulses bound anew,
And turned to him – nor breeze, nor ray
Revived that mound of shattered clay,
Scarce conscious of his pain he lay –
Scarce conscious that my hands removed
The glittering toys his lightness loved;
The jewelled rings, and locket fair
Where rival curls of silken hair,
Sable and brown, revealed to me
A tale of doubtful constancy.

'Forsake the world without regret,'
I murmured in contemptuous tone;
'The world, poor wretch, will soon forget
'Thy noble name, when thou art gone!
'Happy, if years of slothful shame
'Could perish like a noble name –
'If God did no account require
'And being with breathing might expire!'

And words of such contempt I said,
Harsh insults o'er a dying bed
Which as they darken memory now
Disturb my pulse and flush my brow.
I know that Justice holds in store,
Reprisals for those days of gore;
Not for the blood, but for the sin
Of stifling mercy's voice within.

The blood spilt gives no pang at all;
It is my conscience haunting me,
Telling how oft my lips shed gall
On many a thing too weak to be
Even in thought my enemy;
And whispering ever, when I pray,
'God will repay – God will repay!'

He does repay, and soon and well,
The deeds that turn his earth to hell,
The wrongs that aim a venomed dart
Through nature at the Eternal Heart.
Surely my cruel tongue was cursed;
I know my prisoner heard me speak;
A transient gleam of feeling burst
And wandered o'er his haggard cheek,
And from his quivering lids there stole
A look to melt a demon's soul,
A silent prayer more powerful far
Than any breathed petitions are,
Pleading in mortal agony
To mercy's Source but not to me.

Now I recall that glance and groan,
And wring my hands in vain distress;
Then I was adamantine stone,
Nor felt one touch of tenderness.

My plunder ta'en I left him there,
Without one breath of morning air,
To struggle with his last despair,
Regardless of the wildered cry
Which wailed from death, yea wailed to die.

I left him there unwatched, alone,
And eager sought the court below,
Where o'er a trough of chizelled stone
An ice cold well did gurgling flow.

The water in its basin shed
A stranger tinge of fiery red,
I drank and scarcely marked the hue –
My hand was dyed with crimson too.

As I went out a ragged child,
With wasted cheek and ringlets wild,
A shape of fear and misery,
Raised up her helpless hands to me,
And begged her father's . . . to see.
I spurned the piteous wretch away;
'Thy father's . . . is lifeless clay,
'As thine mayst be ere fall of day,
'Unless the truth be quickly told –
'Where they have hid thy father's gold.'
Yet through the intervals of pain
He heard my taunts and moaned again;
And mocking moans did I reply,
And asked him why he would not die

In noble agony – uncomplaining.
Was it not foul disgrace and shame
To thus disgrace his ancient name?
Just then one came hurrying in,
'Alas!' he cried, 'Sin genders sin!

'For every soldier slain they've sworn
'To hang up five ere morn!
'They've ta'en of stragglers sixty-three,
'Full thirty from one company,
'And all my father's family;
'And comrade thou hadst only one;
'They've ta'en thy all – thy little son!'

Down, at my captive's feet I fell:
I had no option in despair:
'As thou wouldst save thy soul from hell,
'My heart's own darling bid them spare,
'Or human hate and hate divine
'Blight every orphan flower of thine!'

He wakened up – he almost smiled:
'I lost last night my only child.
'Twice in my arms, twice on my knee,
'You stabbed my child and laughed at me;
'And so' – with choking voice he said –
'I trust in God – I hope she's dead.
'Yet not to thee, not even to thee,
'Would I return such misery.
'Write that they harm no infant there.
'Write that it is my latest prayer.'

I wrote – he signed – and thus did save
My treasure from the gory grave;
And oh! my soul longed wildly then
To give his saviour life again.

But heedless of my gratitude
The silent corpse before me lay;
And still methinks, in gloomy mood,
I see it fresh as yesterday;
The sad eyes raised imploringly
To mercy's God and not to me.

I could not rescue him; his child
I found alive and tended well;
But she was . . . anguish wild,
And hated me like . . . hell;
And weary with her savage woe
One moonless night I let her go.

14 September 1846

Index of Titles

Index of First Lines

POEMS

Feasts and Fasts

Christina Rossetti

Christina Rossetti (1830–1894) was born in London of Italian parents. With her vivid imagination and innate talent for composing verse, she was an accomplished poet by her late teens. By the mid 1850s her brother Dante Gabriel had become one of the leaders of the Pre-Raphaelite brotherhood, giving Christina the opportunity to publish poetry in the brotherhood's magazine. By 1866 she was established as a leading poet of her day.

Prematurely in 1871 she was stricken with Graves Disease, becoming increasingly preoccupied with the relationship between earth and heaven, life and death. She had inherited a devout Anglican faith from her mother, and from this point on her verse became almost entirely religious. Two of her most religious poems – 'In the Bleak Mid-winter' and 'Love Came Down at Christmas' – have since been set to music as carols.

This volume focuses on her poetry marking the feasts and fasts of the Christian year. Divided into sections including Advent, Christmas, Lent and Easter, it is designed to be dipped into at the appropriate times, an aid to gentle reflection throughout the year.

POEMS AND DEVOTIONS

John Donne

John Donne was born in 1572 and, a Roman Catholic in his youth, took Anglican Orders in 1615 and was Dean of St Paul's from 1621 until his death.

His poetry, though forgotten for a long period, is the finest example of the so-called 'metaphysical' style – learned, allusive and witty. It is both highly physical and highly spiritual, with no distinction in method or content between the sacred and secular poems, both of which are included in this anthology.

Less well-known, but equally compelling, are his early *Devotions upon Emergent Occasions*, meditations and prayers issuing from a profound trust in God.

As Dean of St Paul's, Donne gained the reputation of being the finest preacher in the land; his use of strong rhythms and striking images made for powerful sermons. This volume contains edited versions of five of these, including the classic 'Death's Duel'.

THE COMPLETE POEMS

with selected prose

Gerard Manley Hopkins

Gerard Manley Hopkins (1844–1889) was born into a devout Anglican family in Stratford, Essex, and converted to Catholicism in his final year at Oxford. He became a member of the Society of Jesus and was ordained in 1877. After some years as a priest, he became a professor of Classics at University College, Dublin, but died from typhoid four years later at the age of forty-five.

He displayed remarkable poetic creativity throughout his life, though on becoming a Jesuit found this ability difficult to reconcile with religious devotion. Through the teaching of Duns Scotus he came to recognize the importance of allowing individual talent, and hence his poetic gifts, to be exercised in the service of the Church. Sadly, his poetry was rejected for publication in his lifetime, though in later years it was regarded as innovative and highly influential.

Hopkins is best known for his nature mysticism, exploring the revelation of the divine within the natural world. This complete collection of his surviving verse is complemented by a selection of extracts from his notebooks and sermons, specially chosen to reveal the essence of his mystical vision.

MY CONFESSION

Leo Tolstoy

Leo Tolstoy's literary stature rests almost entirely on his two master-pieces, *Anna Karenina* and *War and Peace*. Less well known are his books on moral and religious themes for which he was dubbed 'the conscience of the continent' in his day. These books were inspired by his mid-life conversion to the Christian faith.

His approach to Christianity was quite distinct. He disliked the dogma, insisting on the simple, practical truths of Jesus' teaching and emphasizing the importance of the individual conscience in upholding these truths. He saw that spiritual insight was often granted to the simple and uneducated in society, prompting a radical change in his own lifestyle.

Written immediately after his conversion and widely praised by his contemporaries, *My Confession* traces the development of Tolstoy's faith and morality. It is an absorbing account of the influences on his life and literature. In a frank, autobiographical style, he reveals the complex intellectual, moral and spiritual turmoil which brought him to the brink of suicide, and the faith through which he eventually attained, to some degree, a peace of mind.

THE PILGRIM'S PROGRESS

John Bunyan

Written in prison, where Bunyan had been sent for unauthorized preaching, and first published in 1678, this classic story has been described as the most popular work of Christian spirituality written in English, and as the first English novel. It describes the road to the Celestial City, by way of Doubting Castle, the Delectable Mountains, Vanity Fair and other places whose names have entered the very fabric of the language.

Fascinating as literature, entertaining as story, profound as spiritual teaching for the soul's journey, *The Pilgrim's Progress* is 'a masterpiece which generation after generation of ordinary men and women have taken to their hearts'.

HUGH ROSS WILLIAMSON